✳ ❧ ✳ ❧ ✳ ❧ ✳ ❧ ✳ ❧ ✳ ❧ ✳ ❧ ✳ ❧ ✳ ❧ ✳ ❧ ✳ ❧ ✳ ❧ ✳

FINAL STOP!
BINGE EATING

Simple Methods and Strategies to Maintain Mindful Eating and enjoy it's benefits

✳ ❧ ✳ ❧ ✳ ❧ ✳ ❧ ✳ ❧ ✳ ❧ ✳ ❧ ✳ ❧ ✳ ❧ ✳ ❧ ✳

Cathrine Kowal

Table of Contents

Introduction

If you're reading this, you're looking for information on eating disorders that you couldn't find on Google.

Unfortunately, we live in a society that promotes thinness as some warped standard of beauty, which is particularly odd, seeing as Americans continue to gain more and more weight than usual even while being so concerned about their weight as often as they have the time to. For some people, this happens every 5 minutes.

Before I jump right into binge eating, let's take a look at the umbrella it falls under - eating disorders. Eating disorders are usually taken to extremes, which lead to strange eating behaviors that inevitably affect their well-being and not positively. There are three main types of eating disorders. I'll list and explain briefly, just surface knowledge.

Patients with **anorexia nervosa** have warped mental and even physical images of their physical bodies. This disorder pushes them to want to shed this 'weight' even when it is obviously nonexistent. Well, obvious to everyone but them. This results in compulsive workouts, starving for dangerous periods of time, skipping meals often, or even plain refusal to eat in front of people.

Patients with **bulimia nervosa** are in a completely different circle of their own. They actually eat, even in large amounts, but then go ahead to rid their bodies of whatever they consumed in any way possible. Some would rather purge, others would just use enemas, diuretics, compulsive exercising, laxatives, and vomiting. Some others would go through all these options to eventually settle for the most effective at the time.

People with **binge eating disorder** go through out-of-control eating episodes just like people with bulimia nervosa. Technically, they eat like maniacs, but the difference between the disorders is that binge eaters don't feel the need to get rid of the calories by vomiting or purging. They don't really care about the calories. I'm not sure they even notice.

Just a quick note - there are certain eating disorders that don't quite fit the bill for binge eating, anorexia, or bulimia, but that doesn't change the fact that they are eating disorders. They just don't have a finite category just yet. The point of all this jargon is awareness and prevention of unusual behavior that will inevitably lead to an eating disorder. Take bulimia and anorexia for example; these usually start with strict weight loss programs or even stricter dieting. Binge eating is usually preceded by basic bingeing every once in a while. A cookie today, a croissant tomorrow. However, once these occasional behaviors start negatively affecting a person's physical and mental health, it is time to pay a visit to the psychologist.

Particularly one trained in the causes and treatments of eating disorders

Who Should Be Worried?

The National Institute of Mental Health says that these problems mainly plague the female population, but like it or not, males are affected too. It's easy to assume that men aren't as bothered about their image as women since they're automatically expected to be less fragile and trivial, but men are just as vulnerable.

Studies show that over a quarter of adolescent anorexia cases happen to boys. Families and friends may never suspect a person with an eating disorder mostly because these people understand the abnormality of their behavior and therefore engage in secret. They can also go as far as severing social ties and even denying the problematic nature of their eating habits. One can and should be diagnosed only by a trained psychologist or mental health professional.

Causes of Eating Disorders

Certain personality traits and psychological factors can make a person more likely to engage in bad eating habits. Issues like feelings of helplessness, distorted body image, and low self-esteem can predispose a person to eating disorders. However, certain traits have been linked to specific disorders. Anorexia, for example, usually plagues perfectionists, while bulimic people are almost always impulsive. Genetic factors are also involved, but I won't go into that today.

Certain situations that can give rise to eating disorders are

- Bullying

- Repeated body shaming by friends and family.

- Inability to participate in certain physical activities due to weight.

- Negative feelings or post-traumatic stress from abuse, losing a loved one, and even rape.

- Oddly enough, happy moments.

These factors are major contributors to the likelihood of eating disorders because of the mental and physical stress that comes with these life events and how they affect the physical appearance of a person.

All you need to do is start, and the disorder will quite literally take it from there, putting you in an endless cycle of eating away your life problems and probably purging then stuffing your face again the next time you have a crisis. Binge eating is one of the mighty three, but unlike its partners, it doesn't really give 0ff red flags until you're neck-deep. I'll explain it a little bit.

Let's say you're on a popular talk show, and the theme today is "Food romance: dealing with your hot and cold relationship with food." If you're still in college, I think it's safe to agree that you love to eat but somehow hate the dormitory meals. Instead, you find yourself stuffing your face with cafeteria food.

Remember that night you ordered a pizza right after a major meal, and before a big day? You know you weren't hungry; you were stress eating, and instead of telling yourself this, you rather believed you couldn't decide on what to eat so you 'mindlessly' snacked on a lot of junk today and proper food, the next.

You claimed to worry about it, so instead of dealing with the problem head-on, you punish yourself by going through grueling exercise routines and dieting, but guess who ordered two boxes of pizza the same night just because… Exactly!

If all that seems even vaguely familiar, then congratulations, you have firsthand experience with bingeing. Unfortunately for you, you seem to be a bit of an expert on complicated food relationships, so you're on a talk show to share your unrivaled wisdom and experience on the subject.

Now the programs continue after a short commercial break, and the host looks you straight in the eye and says, "*I honestly wonder why binge eating is such a major problem for you. You spend a lot of time checking calories, worrying about cellulite, but still stuffing your face every chance you get. Make us understand*"

She hit the nail on the head, didn't she? You have tried so hard to get out of the endless cycle of binge eating by drowning in diet books and articles, but after a few days or once there's a crisis, you fall headfirst into your bad habits again. Did dieting help even a little bit? Did it make you feel happier? Clearly, not so why do you look to dieting for some form of control?

Don't feel alone; everyone here today can relate to your binge eating dilemma. They all understand the delicate line between eating too little and eating too much. There is a more delicate line between loving your body and hating it.

A lot of people take that first step across the line into binge eating during their college days, and unfortunately for them, those first steps can be very definitive of their eating pattern years into the future. Now, what would you tell the host and audience?

Will you confess to being a binge eater hoping for a wonder-working diet routine that will automatically take off the pounds that you will eventually gain because **you just can't stop?** Do you feel a stab of guilt every time you cheat on your diet with your favorite meals or snacks? Do you have reasons to wonder if you even have an eating disorder?

If you have ever harbored thoughts like these, then better don't stop reading because I have your miracle cure right here. If you're still not sure if you have a binge eating problem, go through the list below quickly before we carry on.

- Do you overeat until you feel too full?

- Do you eat whenever you are under any kind of pressure? For example, munching on a bag of nuts while preparing a report that is due in about two hours.

- Are you terrified of putting on the pounds?

- Ever caught yourself thinking too much about food?

- Do you skip meals because you feel you're too busy, and instead, you eat a lot of junk on the go?

- Have you ever wondered if you have a toxic relationship with food?

- Have you tried and failed to go on a diet?

- Have you ever truly felt fat?

- Have you ever experienced weight fluctuations that are not caused by an underlying health problem?

- Have you ever said out loud, "I think I am fat"?

Chapter 1

Binge Eating 101

Bingeing is a word that used to mean a particular thing to the majority; excessive drinking. Now, the word is more widely used to refer to eating excessively. To a lot of people, bingeing is something as inconsequential as a basic overindulgence or a simple dietary lapse. To others, it is a total or partial loss of the control one has overconsumption. This is a bigger problem than most people realize, and it's not particular to the westerners. Despite being a major problem that is undeniably popular, a lot of people know very little about it.

Is purging always preceded by bingeing? Is this a lifelong health problem? Can it be fixed? Is it a sign of something much worse? How can we tell the difference between a simple overindulgence and true bingeing? What makes a person predisposed to binge eating? How can I fix it?

These are very important questions that most people ask.

The Meaning of the Word 'Binge'

The definition of 'binge' has evolved over the years. It was widely used in the nineteenth century, and it meant 'a heavy drinking spree,' and it remains one of the definitions you will find in the Oxford English Dictionary. The other definitions influenced by modern times, include overindulgence or overeating.

According to the eleventh edition of Merriam Webster's Collegiate Dictionary, bingeing is basically an unrestrained indulgence or overindulgence. This indulgence has been reported by men and women. For some, it starts out as an occasional binge, which remains an occasional binge that has no negative effect on their lives. For others, it progresses into a major problem that starts to affect many areas of their lives negatively. The reason a lot of people can't distinguish the two is the similarities between the two and the ignorance of people with regards to the behavior.

Due to this confusion, research has been conducted into the experiences of binge eaters and while all accounts aren't exactly the same, there are two very distinct features that were found common among binge eaters - the amount of food consumed is seen as excessive by the eater not necessarily an outsider, and they all seem to lose control during the indulgence. So when trying to identify a binge, check if the food being consumed is obviously more than what others would have under the same circumstances.

Characteristics of a Binge

I read somewhere about a girl that said she would randomly select whatever food she could get her hands on and just stuff her face with it sometimes without chewing it. After some minutes, she would start to feel guilty and scared because her stomach would start to ache, but she wouldn't be able to stop. She complained about a rise in temperature and how she would only be able to stop eating when she felt really sick. Going through personal accounts of binge eating can be a real eye-opener. Let's take a look at certain spot-on traits of a true binge.

1. **Feelings:** The first few moments of a binge can feel like heaven as it should be since you repeat it every single time you feel the need to, which is a lot if we're honest. The feeling and taste of the food on your tongue will feel so intense and pleasurable. However, these feelings vanish as quickly as they came and are immediately replaced by feelings of guilt and disgust as you continue to stuff your face uncontrollably. This is very common among binge eaters. They feel repulsed by their actions, yet they continue to eat.

2. **Consumption Speed:** Binge eaters are not very slow eaters. It is typically a rapid process. They stuff their faces as if on auto-pilot sometimes without even chewing the food. Others push the food down their throats with drinks, particularly sodas, and this is another major reason they feel full and heavy really quickly. For people with bulimia, drinking too much makes it easier to throw up later.

3. **Agitation:** It's a common habit for binge eaters to wander around or pace their environment while they eat. It's almost like desperation. Some people have described the craving to be some kind of powerful force that makes them eat, and this is the reason compulsive eating and binge eating can be used interchangeably. This isn't the only behavior of agitation they exhibit. Some might go as far as taking food that doesn't belong to them, shoplift or even consume food that has been discarded just to satisfy a craving. Guess what happens right after… Feelings of disgust, degradation and shame.

Allow me to paint a quick picture. You start by having a bowl of oatmeal, which you eat as quickly as you can and move on to have three or four extra bowls. By now, you should know that your control has flown with the wind, and you're already knee-deep in bingeing but you can't seem to help yourself. You feel very tense during the desperate search for anything to eat. Anything at all. You run around looking for discarded food even while acknowledging how disgusting that is. Luckily for you, you find some and wolf them down quickly. Other times, you decide to go into town to 'check out' stores and do a bit of grocery shopping.

Just enough to not seem like a shoplifter when, in fact, you **are** shoplifting because the amount of money you have won't be enough to buy what you need to satisfy your cravings. Now you eat and eat until you physically can't anymore. See what I mean?

4. **Trance-like state:** Some people have described the binge to feel like they're stuck in a trance, almost like their behavior is being remotely controlled. If you have had an experience just like this, you understand when I say that it feels like you're not exactly the one eating.

   Some people also claim to engage in some other activity like listening to very loud music or reading a book **while** bingeing because it distracts them from what they're actually doing, which pretty much prevents them from owning up to their bad habit. I'll paint a picture. You wake up with that feeling in your stomach, maybe someone upset you deeply yesterday, or you're just sad, you feel this overwhelming urge to binge. Almost immediately, you begin to feel clammy and hot, and then your mind goes dark. You make your way towards the food and dig in quickly, scared that you might start to think and feel guilty if you eat slowly.

   In fact, you get up and pace while you eat or watch a series, anything distracting enough to keep your mind off what you're doing because once you have enough time to think about the fact that you're bingeing, you might even feel sadder because it's a reminder that you have a bad habit. Seem familiar?

5. **Secrets:** A typical binge happens in secret because of the shame that is attached to the habit. Some people feel so much shame that drives them to hide it for as long as they can; months and even years. The most basic way they do this is to eat as normally as possible when in the presence of

others. Do you eat normally during a family meal or around friends then go back much later to swallow all the leftovers? Do you sneak food into your bedroom so you can indulge with zero fear of getting caught? Do you go shopping for food right after work and eat more than half of it in the privacy of your car before you get home?

Doing this reduces any chance of getting help because even with all the disgust and shame you feel afterward, you do it again and again and again because you honestly don't know any other effective way.

6. **Losing Control:** Like I have said earlier, losing control is one of the major features of bingeing. It is what makes normal overeating different from bingeing. This particular characteristic of the habit varies between individuals.

   Some have said they feel it way before the bingeing even starts; others have said it slowly builds while they eat, and others have said that it kicks in immediately they realize just how much they have eaten.

   An interesting thing to note is that a lot of people who have been bingeing for years claim that the loss of control has diminished over the years because they became comfortable with the fact that their binges are lifelong - so they don't even try to fight the urge anymore.

   Others even plan into the future for what they perceive as inevitable binges, which automatically adds some extra cushion to their comfy chair of bad habits but on the plus side, this method gives them a certain amount of control over where the binges happen and availability of food thereby saving them from a lot of uncomfortable and shameful ways of satisfying the craving. You're probably smiling at this because it seems like a reasonable way to manage binge eating, but I assure you, it is not.

It is easy to assume a sense of control when the impact of bingeing is a bit reduces because you 'planned ahead,' but if you were really in control, wouldn't you decide not to binge and actually **not** binge? Control should be the ability to prevent a recurrence. Besides, a lot of people still eat until they feel physically sick because of the inability to stop.

You might say you take breaks like the time you had to take an important call or you had a visitor but be very honest, didn't you go right back when the distraction was gone? My point exactly.

Diagnosing Binge Eating Disorder

People clearly differ in what they binge on and how often they do it, so it is quite difficult to diagnose a binge based on those two factors alone, but let's look at those factors with a sprinkle of individuality and see how a proper diagnosis should be made.

1. **Duration and Frequency:** Before you are diagnosed with binge eating disorder or bulimia nervosa, which are just two of the three major eating disorders, you have to binge at least once a week on average.

However, this theory isn't accepted by everyone because it basically exonerates binge eater who indulges less frequently or intermittently. For this reason, some mental health professionals usually ignore this threshold when diagnosing a patient. Instead, they focus on the regularity of the binges and the effects it has on the physical and mental health of the person involved. The importance of frequency is also a bit confusing. What if you only binge once in a while? Does this automatically mean you're in the clear? At what frequency does this become an issue? Is it how often, over what time span, and for how long you indulge that finally determines if you have an eating disorder or how serious it is? Or is it how much it negatively affects the quality of your life that finally does it? As I have mentioned earlier, professionals are usually concerned about how badly the disorder has affected the quality of life. How long binges last usually depends on whether or not a person has the intention of vomiting right after, as seen in bulimia nervosa. Research conducted in Oxford has shown that binges last about two hours in people who do not vomit and about half that time in people who do. This has been attributed to the fact that people who throw up after feeling pressure to satisfy the cravings as quickly as possible so they can get rid of the excess before absorption begins.

2. **Foods consumed:** The foods most likely eaten during an episode include chocolate, jam, cereal, cake, condensed milk, or some improvised sweet food like cake batter.

Basically, food that is pretty easy to get hands-on and eat. Food that needs very little or no preparation. You might not eat any of these on a craving free day because of how fattening they are but when you start to get that feeling in your stomach, it's almost like you just can't eat enough. Statistics have shown that people who binge usually have two kinds of replies when asked the kind of food they binge on. The first reply usually has to do with the food character so they are likely to say, 'filling food' or 'sweet food.' The second reply has to do with their various attitudes towards the food so they are likely to say, 'fattening food' or 'dangerous food.' The main thing to be noted here is that most people binge on foods that they are likely to avoid on a normal day. This is crucial to the comprehension of the causes and permanent treatment of binge eating. A popular myth about binges is that they are mostly food rich in carbohydrates. The truth, however, is that the carbohydrate content in binge foods are almost the same with normal meals if not lower. The main feature of binge foods has nothing to do with their fat, protein or carb content. Instead, it has everything to do with the total amount consumed. If you binge, you most likely eat cookies, ice cream, cake, etc. but just like Timothy Walsh has said, the widespread belief that these foods have a high carb content is false. Instead, they are simply sweet foods that contain a lot of fat.

Also, due to the evolution of science and more discoveries, the whole carb craving craze has been proven to be false because binge foods are composed of foods that are seen as 'forbidden' by the binge eater. So it can be carbs, fat or even protein. It all depends on the individual.

Different Kinds of Binges

This is most likely the first time you're seeing this, right? This is so much deeper than what the average person knows. It is easier to grasp the idea of binge eating, but now there are types? It is not strange for a person to claim to have more than one binge eating disorder.

Even though all three types may not fit the basic definition of bingeing as we know it, studies have shown that binge eaters describe experiencing these kinds of binges:

- **A Full-blown Binge:** During this kind of binge, food is consumed in insane amounts and very quickly without pleasure except for the first wave of pleasure you get when the food first touches your tongue. Even that is swept away by guilt. It is usually done in secret and a particular place, for example, your kitchen, college dorm, apartment etc. This is the kind of binge eating where laxatives tag along. Right after an episode, you're usually wracked with panic and you feel bloated. Give it a few minutes and that's when the guilt kicks in, and everything else intensifies.

- **A Half Binge:** These ones share some similarities with a full binge apart from the fact that these occur way into the night as quickly as possible in just once place with zero pleasure and oddly enough, zero panic. These are the ones that feel automated, usually as a reaction to a particular situation. The urges are much easier to resist.

- **Slow-mo Binges:** These ones happen at home, not at work or at school. You can actually sense them coming from afar and even attempt to resist for a bit, but you know it won't last, and you find yourself snacking almost compulsively feeling a jolt of pleasure when you start, and this lasts well into the binge. You enjoy this binge because you get to choose foods that you like but do everything to avoid. You might actually take some time to prepare the food for this binge. See why this is the slow-mo version? Anyway, like all binges, the guilt kicks in, and you start to feel terrible, but guess who doesn't stop eating? That's right! You.

That said, some people have very specific binge types that don't fall under any of the categories above. Take some people with anorexia nervosa, for example; they are prone to little subjective binges which share the lack of control and deep distress of a typical objective binge. The binges of people who look obviously overweight are not as easy to put a finger on because they typically last longer than the bulimic binges.

How a Binge Is Born

When I first discovered bingeing, I was so confused by its existence because I couldn't understand why something like that was so recurrent despite the feelings of shame and guilt attached to it. This brings up two important questions:

- What births the binge?

- What keeps it alive?

We'll be taking a look at certain situations that trigger a typical binge. A binge can be triggered by a variety of factors. Some research performed a while ago pointed out the main binge triggers while a more recent study focused on the location of these binges. We'll begin with the triggers:

Some research conducted on 32 people with binge eating disorder in a clinic in Australia yielded the following results concerning their triggers:

1. Tension: 91%

2. Specific food cravings: 78%

3. The feeling of boredom and loneliness: 59%

4. The desire to chew on something: 84%

5. Having intense thoughts about food: 75%

6. Being alone: 78%

7. Going home after a long day at work or school: 72%

Another study focused on thirty-three women with bingeing problems. These women were given laptops for a week and were questioned at intervals about their mood and eating habits. It was recorded that their urges were aroused when they were alone in specific places like:

1. The living room: 31%

2. At work: 10%

3. Kitchen: 31%

4. The car: 10%

Now we will take a look at more detailed triggers:

- **Undereating and The Hunger That Follows:** Some binge eaters, usually the ones with bulimia nervosa and anorexia, don't eat so much when they're not bingeing. This food deprivation mostly yields harmful effects seeing as it is pretty much the same as starvation. Nobody really likes starved to the best of my knowledge. Placing rigid boundaries on feeding and eating as little as possible can negatively affect a person psychologically and physiologically so much that when they finally begin to eat, it takes a lot of willpower to stop - willpower that they hardly ever possess. Think of it like a dam being burst open. A lot binge eaters have reported having the urge sometime around midday on that one day they choose not to eat. This self-imposed abstinence equals hunger (a problem), which automatically makes the body want to fix that, thereby initiating the constant thoughts of food. This mental torture can go on and on stretching into the evening, say around 4 pm. At this point, it becomes almost impossible to distract yourself from the images of chips floating around in your head, and up you go straight to McDonald's. The trigger here is hunger. This kind of hunger isn't picky, so instead of eating a normal meal to quell it, you find yourself eating whatever you can lay your hands on, and this feeling isn't partial to things you don't like. YOU WANT IT ALL!

- **Breaking A Dietary Rule:** This might shock you, but a lot of binge eaters are dieters, and their dieting is usually stricter than the regular one you're used to. They follow every single dietary rule to the T starting with what to eat when to eat and the amount to eat. This usually starts off as a bingeing treatment plan, but it all turns to dust when they break even one rule. Everything almost always comes flooding.

- **Alcohol:** A lot of people have come to realize that alcohol is not a friend when it comes to fixing a binge eating disorder. There are many plausible explanations for this. First of all, drinking too much alcohol will get you drunk or mentally impaired. By the way, too much alcohol varies per person, and it depends solely on the individual threshold. Back to how drunkenness can affect your 'bye-bye binge' plan, your judgment will be obviously affected, and whatever resistance you had against the binges will slowly dissolve as the alcohol kicks in. Let's say you planned to eat just salad at a friend's party; alcohol will make you think it's okay to eat a few extra things because of impaired judgment, a major feature of alcohol. Also, excessive alcohol makes some people depressed and sad, imagine the results on a binge eater.

- **Unpleasant emotions:** Feelings of sadness, frustration, and depression can kick start a binge. Depression is more powerful than most people realize. Bingeing can begin whenever you're tired or just plain upset, these feelings bring about emptiness, and you might honestly try to resist the urge to binge, but it only gets as intense as whatever you might be feeling at that moment. The only way out for you is to eat which makes total sense because eating is quite a distraction. The only problem with your kind of eating is the feelings of self-criticism and guilt that washes over you after. Stress, feelings of hopelessness, anger, tension, anxiety, and irritability are also very powerful emotional triggers.

- **Absence Of Time Structure:** Unstructured time during the day can predispose a person to binge eating because, at some point, you might have a lot of excess time with little or no plans and remember what I said about boredom? Routines are your best friend in times like this because you'll always have a distraction at every point in time, and before you know it, it's bedtime, and you didn't binge even once!

- **Being Alone:** Because binges mostly take place in secret, finding yourself all alone for long periods will most likely tempt your binge monster. Being alone is very difficult from loneliness in that one can be surrounded by people and still feel lonely, but both situations increase the risks of binge eating.

- **Feeling Fat:** This particular trigger has been reported mostly by women. This doesn't mean that it has zero effects on men; it's just a woman thing. Surprisingly, this feeling is more common amongst people with an eating disorder. For them, this feeling is almost always equated with being overweight regardless of their actual body size, and because most people are uncomfortable with weight gain, they feel sad, which automatically makes them binge to distract themselves.

- **Actual Weight Gain:** This, unlike the previous trigger, is not a delusion. The automatic response to weight gain is almost always negative even for weight gain as tiny as a pound. This causes a whole different kind of frustration, especially for bulimic binge eaters and dieters. The most-reported response to this is giving up any weight control attempts they might have been making. They fall headfirst into bingeing. Sometimes, this might have even been a teeny tiny misunderstanding with your weighing scale. You see, bodyweight is never steady all through the day because of certain factors like hydration.

- **Premenstrual Syndrome (PMS):** These are dangerous times for every woman. The mood swings peak, bloating kicks in, the cramping starts, and the food cravings follow suit. Binge eaters have complained about the irresistible urge to binge a few days to their period. Irresistible being the keyword. This is pretty much unavoidable and is usually due to factors like the cramps and mood swings. A major trigger here.

The Link Between Obesity and Binge Eating

The definition of obesity is relative. An anorexic person will most likely define it as any weight gain as little as four pounds. The average grandmother might think she's obese because she weighs 165 pounds on her muscular large-boned self. In the modeling world, obesity might mean 135 pounds on a 5"10 body. See the different angles here? These women are not medically obese. In fact, the model and anorexic are grossly underweight. People have very different opinions about weight. A lot of people are bothered by a few pounds, while others are perfectly fine with being on the large side.

However, science says a person is obese when they weigh a little over 20% of the weight, particular to their height, age, and body type. A person is only morbidly obese when they weigh over a hundred pounds above the expected weight for their body type, age, and height. Currently, healthy weight has made room for a few extra pounds per height than what was originally expected. This is due to some research that has found a connection to low mortality rate and more weight than is currently seen as 'fashionable.'

Research conducted a while back by the Center for Disease Control and Prevention proves that about 62% percent of the adults in America are medically overweight. In the 62%, 35% are just moderately overweight while the rest are totally obese. Also, they also discovered that 13% of children living in the U.S. are grossly overweight. Different government research released in October 2002 states that 31% of the American population is grossly overweight. It also indicated that about 15% of people between 6 and 19 years are obese, and that's not all. 10% of toddlers are really overweight.

Okay, let's say all that research was conducted years ago. How about more recent ones that state that over 31% of teen girls in America and shy of 28% of teen boys are overweight. An extra 14% of boys and 15% of girls are totally obese. The causes? Let's see; Fast food, a lot of time spent in front of the computer or smartphone, snack with an insane amount of fat and sugar, and our overall winner…

Bingeing! And because of this particular cause, obesity is on the rise in all ethnic and major socioeconomic groups across the world

What Built The Binge-Obesity Bridge?

1. **Eating more calories than you burn:** I think I should point something out really quick. Not all binge eaters are overweight because luckily, for some, they get to burn the

excess calories through workouts, work, and other things. Back in the 1990s, people in the U.S. ate a whopping 340 extra calories than they had in the 80s and roughly 500 calories extra than they consumed in the 50s. Calorie consumption has been on the rise for a while now, especially with the introduction of refined carbs mixed with saturated fat. These foods are seen as unhealthy and therefore forbidden to most and that is exactly the kind of food the same people binge on. Doing this without a sure way to let those calories go is definitely going to lead to obesity and by letting the calories go, I don't mean purging.

2. **Introduction of fast food:** Americans eat out more now than they usually do in the past, partly because fast food joints and restaurants dish out more portions than some people are used to and partly because it's easier and quicker. A lot of families have takeout for dinner these days, which can be a blessing sometimes when you consider time and energy levels at the end of every day. However, on the other side of things, these fast foods have made bingeing a breeze. Want to binge but don't have the energy actually to do anything? Easy, order a box of pizza or three. Most people have absolutely no idea what is contained in the meals they purchase on the go, so there's a good chance they are packed with lots of sugar and unhealthy saturated fat, unlike a home-cooked meal where you can actually decide what goes in the pot and what doesn't. Convenience is winning, guys. A pack of home-delivered chips and a goods series seems

like the life until you realize your clothes stop fitting. Don't get me started on the health risks of obesity.

3. **The easy way out of emotional pain:** People eat for a lot of reasons outside hunger. Reasons like sadness, depression, and loneliness. These can quickly pack on the pounds if you don't find a better outlet for your emotions.

4. **Prolonged diets and starvation:** I'm sure I have mentioned this before. When you go on a very strict diet plan to make your body slimmer than genetically possible, it starts to fight back by demanding more food than you'd rather consume, and this makes you very vulnerable to bingeing and regaining the weight you tried so hard to lose plus extra. Studies claim that over 90% of dieters put on all the weight they lost with a nice 10 pounds on top in a span of five years. It's a never-ending cycle. Lose the weight and get it all back plus extra when your body can't take it anymore. See how this can make you obese?

5. **It's biological:** This might seem unfair, but it is the truth; some people are really obese because of biological problems that they have little to no control over. Problems like a faulty pituitary or thyroid gland. Other obese people might be physically impaired, so they have no way of shedding the excess calories. The worst part is having any of these biological impairments **and** an eating disorder. Research published in 2003 in the New England Medical Journal

states that the development of binge eating and obesity rely on certain genetic processes.

6. **Stress eating:** There's brand new research that states that there's a connection between the urge to eat and stress. This bridge is also known as **comfort foods**. They usually contain a lot of fat, calories, and sugar. They are called comfort foods because they somehow manage to relax the body in moments of extreme stress. Another important thing to note is that the stimulation of fat cells is greatly encouraged by stress. The world now is highly competitive, demanding, and very fast-paced. This automatically leads to a drastic increase in stress and a high demand for comfort foods, which eventually leads to overeating, being overweight, and obesity in that exact order.

Chapter 2

How Common Is
Binge Eating Disorder?

Bingeing is three times as widespread as bulimia nervosa and anorexia combined, and like it or not, about 40% of the affected population is male. Another thing that might shock you is the lack of studies on binge eating compared to other eating disorders. It was just listed among mental disorders in 2013. A lot of the research already conducted is focused on helping people with weight loss, which is a bit counterproductive because weight loss journeys are one of the major causes of binge eating. Dieting as a form of treatment will only further establish the eating disorder, especially when food is used as an escape from uncomfortable feelings. Certain people who advocate for eating disorders have come to the conclusion that weight stigma is the real reason why there aren't a lot of funds going into binge eating. Diet culture has taken up residence in our overall culture and is now a chunk of your beliefs so much that people are judged initially based on their current body size.

Who is at Risk for Binge Eating Disorders?

Due to the fact that binge eating is a form of dissociation, people living with trauma, stress or PTSD are common targets. It is all about escaping the current reality. If you're a binge eater, you understand when I talk about the time you're all the way into the process of bingeing, and it actually feels like you just took a few steps outside the door that is your life, and you're either timelessly munching away, completely focused on the food or nothing at all. Other people at risk include victims of fat-shaming, people with a strong desire to be thin, or a dislike for their body. Weight stigma is very real, remember that.

Yasi Ansari is a national spokesperson for the school of nutrition and dietetics. She also happens to be a registered and experienced dietitian nutritionist. She said that she had encountered a lot of patients with a history of trauma or some difficulty coping with life transitions or negative situations. She noticed it was some kind of coping mechanism or escape route to deal with emotional and mental distress. It is very important in understanding the need for comfort food.

People who are victims of binge eating almost always have a history of strict food restrictions. Sometimes it's as simple as a person who decides to stay away from some food groups; other times, it is as complicated as an anorexia diagnosis. A good example is a person who binges on carbs having a history of failed multiple low-carb diet plans.

Fat shaming and weight stigma is a major problem that people are afraid to talk about despite its obvious harmful effects on the lives of others. It should be written on billboards that physical appearance and gross weight are not part of the criteria for a proper binge eating disorder diagnosis. It seems easy to assume that binge eating is restricted to people with bigger bodies, but that assumption is false. It is also very common in lightweight people as well. Yes, over two-thirds of people currently living with BED are medically obese, but it is not restricted to a particular body type. Some models are major binge eaters, as well.

You may not know this, but every time you fat shame a person or treat larger people any differently than others, you are actually exposing them to trauma, which can lead to binge eating in some or some other coping mechanism in others. Weight stigma is a major cause of eating disorders. People want to get thinner; they start throwing up food after every meal and eventually end up anorexic. Put yourself in the shoes of a person whose body size has been deemed unattractive or wrong or even immoral in the eyes of everyone and tell me that your physical and mental health won't take a proper beating over time. In the end, the goal is to take better care of ourselves and stay as healthy as we can.

Weight shaming is something a lot of people should be educated on because it is a major breeding ground for eating disorders, especially binge eating. Four out of ten patients scouring the web for weight loss treatments are binge eaters.

Most people living with the struggle of binge eating disorder are also dealing with shame. So much shame. A good portion of it is as a result of the disorder itself (i.e., for people who go through the binge-purge cycle), and the other portion usually starts brewing long before the disorder actually sets in, and it is one of those major factors that predispose a person to develop BED. Struggling with shame is equal to struggling with a constant chronic idea of personal inadequacy and a throbbing fear that said inadequacies would leak out for everyone to see, and as a result, you will be completely humiliated and neglected. You have those moments when you dwell on and drown in your shame. In this moment, you judge yourself more harshly than anyone actually ever would and you find yourself lacking and worthless. Shame is that feeling you get when you wish the ground would just bare its jaws and take you as deep as possible. Shame will tell you that everyone else will judge you the exact same you have judged yourself no matter how untrue that is, so in your head, you have already been cast aside by everyone. Shame will amplify your loneliness. Sometimes this kind of shame can be caused by family background and upbringing. Other times it is caused by the environment. Either way, you are more likely to binge eat than your shame-free neighbors.

Nature or Nurture?

I think it is safe to agree that no one thing causes BED. Some say binge eaters are born that way; others say life experiences made them that way. I say it's a little bit of both. Studies have shown how certain environmental and biological factors contribute to the development of binge eating disorder. I'll give a list:

1. **Your biology:** Like it or not, your family background is a major contributor to your risk of binge eating. Apparently, parents who are stress and emotional eaters are likely to give birth to and raise children with the same traits, so if you're a binge eater, maybe there's something about your parents that they don't want you to know.

2. **Childhood abuse:** What I'm about to point out might seem like something out of a Hollywood cliché, but a history of childhood neglect or trauma contributes to the risks of developing BED. This isn't all talk or assumptions, men and women with BED have reported to have survived one childhood traumatic experience or the other, binge eating being the coping mechanism.

3. **Self-esteem:** I've mentioned something very similar if you would just scroll up a little bit. The search for very unrealistic standards with regards to appearance increases the chances of becoming a binge eater. The common targets are adolescents because, at that stage, they are still developing physically and mentally, so societal body ideals get to them much easier than the adult. This will begin a journey to meet these impossible ideals. Failure to meet these goals leads to emotional distress. A lot of BED patients have reported cases of weight shaming early in life by either their mates, teachers, family, or even coaches. This will definitely center their attention on their physical appearance especially at that impressionable age.

4. **Strict dieting:** I have probably over-explained this so you can scroll up for more information, but I'll summarize for those that can't. When a person makes a major effort to restrict calorie intake, which is basically going long periods with no food or labeling certain food groups as forbidden, especially as a remedy for bingeing, all they have achieved is to increase their chances of bingeing. The hunger kicks in, and you're thinking more and more about food before you're fed up just thinking, and you find yourself drowning in food, most likely the ones you labeled forbidden.

5. **Impulsiveness:** Impulsiveness is simply doing then thinking later. If you know any impulsive person, then you've probably been a witness to one of their many moments of regret. People like that respond actively to very powerful emotions, and this puts them at a very high risk of eating the feeling away. The pleasure period for a typical binge is relatively short and despite this, a lot of people still indulge because of how it makes them feel in the moment. That behavior screams impulsiveness. A lot of people have realized how ineffective bingeing is in fixing their problems and this recognition alongside seeking alternative adaptive behaviors are one of the major milestones on the way out of the binge universe. I will give more information on these milestones in a bit. Let's better understand the problem that is step one.

Chapter 3

Ethnicity, Race and Bingeing

Is it Really a Western Thing?

It is assumed that the westernization of non-western ethnic groups and minorities living amongst westerners like the African Americans and Hispanics that is the major cause of the higher occurrence of binge eating among the non-westerners. In simpler terms, a person born and bred in a non-western environment not affected by the western idea of 'thinner is better' might become influenced over time after relocating to a western environment.

Is There a Connection Between Eating Disorders and Race?

Let's take the U.S., for example. Studies have shown that the extent to which an individual adopts the mannerisms and values of a different culture has a strong effect on how high or low the risks of eating disorders will be.

Not everyone accepts this theory of westernization. Some have even pointed out certain places where being overweight is culturally okay, but it does nothing to reduce the prevalence of eating disorders like anorexia. Another good example is the research conducted on Iranian women who migrated to America and Iranian woman living in Iran. Keep in mind that western media is banned in Iran. Moving on, there were more similarities than differences in the levels and intensity of binge eating despite the difference in location and location culture. Also, Iranian women living in Iran seemed more inclined to lose weight and engage in calorie restriction even though the full body-covering doesn't really give a lot of clues about their actual body size. Basically, it's not entirely a western thing.

Are Health Professionals Aware that Non-Westerners have Eating Disorders?

The fact that the theory of westernization isn't accepted by all doesn't affect the key point here, which is that ethnic minorities are also victims of binge eating. Healthcare professionals should be made aware of this because of the results of the research conducted sometime in 1996. I'll tell you a short story.

There were two Latinas, two Native Americans, and two Caucasians. They all had a serious bingeing problem, but the doctors focused all of their resources on the Caucasians because they believed that ethnic minorities couldn't possibly have an eating disorder despite the obvious severity of their symptoms. You see the problem here?

The research proved that the Latinas and Native Americans with obvious binge eating symptoms were less likely to be evaluated by a healthcare professional, unlike the case of the Caucasians. Doctors overlooking ethnic minorities is the major reason a Latina is less likely to seek treatment because she feels she will not be properly attended to. Removing any factor resembling ethnic bias will go a long way in recognizing and properly treating binge eating disorder among minorities, especially minorities where bingeing has been underestimated or simply overlooked. This is another major milestone on the way out of the binge universe.

Why do I know this will work? Native American men began seeking treatment more than halfway into acculturation. They felt comfortable knowing that they would be properly attended to if they acted, behaved, and spoke like Caucasians. How about they start feeling comfortable knowing that they will be properly attended to if they behaved like Native Americans? This includes all the so-called ethnic minorities. Awareness should be made on the acceptance and understanding of cultural differences in relation to binge eating disorder.

Noteworthy Differences between Eating Habits and Reaction to Weight among Major Ethnic Groups in America

Here, I will breeze through the female population of Asian Americans, African Americans, Caucasian Americans, and Hispanic Americans individually.

Caucasian Females

From a general point of view, these females are on level two on a scale of one to ten of body satisfaction, sexual attractiveness, and self-esteem. They are more prone to strict weight control methods than other groups.

Final Stop! **Binge Eating**

Latina Females

These women can be found somewhere in the middle of the scale. They are more satisfied with their bodies and weight than the Caucasians but still go through weight concerns that throw them in the binge eating pit. Some argue that these body image concerns are a result of the pressure from living in a western environment because, in their natural environment, bigger bodies are normally celebrated. These women also have to deal with treatment-seeking struggles for binge eating, especially the stigma that comes with opening up and seeking help.

African American Females

These women scored really high on the self-esteem scale compared to other ethnic groups. They have been observed to be more accepting of their body size, weight, and level of attractiveness despite what their body size might be. They are also not very likely to go through the grueling process of strict calorie restriction. This reason for this general acceptance is the natural flexibility of the African idea of beauty. This is normally very healthy but can also make some oblivious to the high risks of obesity in this group. An interesting fact is that the occurrence of bingeing eating is one of the similarities shared between Latina, Caucasian, and African Americans, despite their different scores on the self-esteem scale. Clearly, body image or weight shaming is not the major reason why African American women binge eat.

Asian American Females

This group seems very different from others with regards to binge eating. Asians undergo so much calorie restriction that it inevitably sets them up for anorexia. Asian Americans from rich and successful families have been observed to be weight perfectionists due to parental expectations. This eventually leads to calorie restriction, which most likely leads to bingeing. Oddly enough, some anorexic Asian Americans are not afraid of being fat. They blame the restrictions on poor appetite and bloating. However, a notable observation was how healthy the anorexic binge eating Asian were compared to their non-Asian peers despite the obvious evidence of the same disorder.

Does a One Size Fit All Approach to Treatment Work?

Some studies have shown that the causes of binge eating differ according to ethnicity, and this has been very helpful in the development of treatment plans.

I'll use cognitive behavioral therapy as an example of one of the many treatment plans for binge eating. This is based on the idea that calorie restriction can cause binge eating, which can also lead to purging.

However, research has shown that the cause of binge eating differs among ethnic groups. Most Caucasians binge eat because of their self-imposed calorie restrictions. Most African Americans binge eat because of peer pressure. Most Latinas binge eat due to anxiety issues.

Interestingly, Latinas usually rely on vomiting as a method of weight control more than the Caucasians, but there still isn't a connection with that and their binge eating habits, unlike Caucasians. This also applies to African Americans, so what this means is that there is no binge-now-purge-later cycle for the African Americans and Latinas. This means that cognitive-behavioral therapy will be more effective on Latinas and African Americans than Caucasians.

However, treatment of binge eating should be relative first before ethnicity, and other factors are taken into consideration.

How Minorities and Eating Disorders are Related

The summary of all the jargon I have been on about is, despite the large body responsible for researching the relationship between 'where you're from' and binge eating, there is still so much to be done and discovered because of the sheer a mouth of factors to be considered. For now, nothing is set in stone about the relationship between ethnicity and bingeing except what I have mentioned so far and the degree of occurrence in ethnic minorities.

I've mentioned this before, but I will do it again for emphasis. Mental health professionals should be informed of the various differences in binge eating causes and symptoms in relation to ethnic groups, so diagnosis and treatment will be easy, thorough, and effective. Now that's all settled, let's move on to the fun part!

Chapter 4

The Science of Binge Eating

Obesity is on the rise in America and other places like Columbia, which is pretty scary because that also means that calorie intake is on the rise. Over time, science has come to understand how hormones affect the human appetite. The discovery of hormones (leptin and ghrelin) responsible for hunger regulation are very crucial in the understanding of expanding waistlines. It is known that hunger and bingeing are not basic functions of human chemistry. They are affected by genes, upbringing, the immediate environment, behavior, attitude, and socialization.

Life changes that are intense enough can biologically affect our hunger levels. Think of it this way, a really sad person might lose appetite partially or completely while an anxious person might be prone to overeating, especially when surrounded by certain smells or sights that have been known to trigger hunger in the past.

Increased and decreased hunger levels are influenced by a series of perfectly structured signaling mechanisms that have been the primary focus of some neuroscience and psychology research.

Binge eating isn't centered on physiology. It is also closely related to psychology, the business of emotions, and behavior. A lot of people struggle with binge eating as a result of verbal injury to their worth or self-esteem. This issue is so deep that there are studies devoted to understanding why this aspect of our lives can't be easily corrected. I mean, it should be as easy as deciding not to stuff your face.

Modern science has come up with a method of mentally processing illnesses and health that is all-encompassing and integrative. There is also a fast-spreading awareness on the causes of binge eating ranging from energy levels throughout the day, hormones, and genes responsible for metabolism, early life, and upbringing to sections of the brain activated by certain sights and smells. Instead of focusing on a particular cause, science has decided to study binge eating as a network of neural systems that work together to affect thought processes, feelings, physiology, and behavior. This disputes a historical theory popular among binge scientists. This idea was to completely blame some carefully selected hormones and neural networks for overeating. This method of simplifying complex processes has been unmatched in science history and is responsible for the many achievements of science. This method has been used in the medical field to identify, breakdown and understand countless illnesses and also come up with viable solutions.

However, there are certain things in nature defy man-made laws and theories based on our understanding of the thing in question. The human body isn't exactly a smartphone with bad parts that can be pinpointed as the reason for its failures. Hunger can be broken down into biological, psychological, and sociological components of human existence. Bingeing is centered on a person's craving and the feeling of not being satisfied according to the levels of dopamine, leptin, and ghrelin released by the brain. Binge eating is more than just a system to be investigated; it is almost deliberate but not quite. It involves the malfunctioning of certain chemical signaling mechanisms in the body and brain.

There are very intricate series of chemical signaling and feedback loops taking place when a person starts to feel hungry even after eating because they are clearly not satisfied. When you feel full, you are not necessarily filled to the brim with food. It is your body's response to glucose levels, dopamine, and a host of other hormones produced by the brain, which lets your body know to continue or stop eating. I'll break it down. Blood sugar levels so are controlled by a hormone called insulin, but not everybody can make this hormone. This hormone is created in and released by the pancreas but some people have a faulty pancreas, which is a condition known as type 1 diabetes. Another blood sugar problem occurs when the pancreas produces insulin just fine but the cells in the body can't quickly pick up this very important hormone. This is called type 2 diabetes.

When the body fails to process blood sugar properly, the formation of fat (adipose tissue) begins. This disordered sugar levels and newly added adipose tissue lead to the production of certain hormones that make a person have intense cravings or not feel full even after a craving was just satisfied.

Fat cells secrete a protein known as leptin that acts as a signaling molecule. In healthy people, this hormone acts to inhibit appetite. One of the causes of obesity is from a failure to produce the right amounts of leptin, but sometimes the problem is more a failure to respond to proper leptin levels.

In the healthy, leptin works in concert with another hormone called ghrelin, which is secreted as a person becomes hungry. After eating, ghrelin levels decline in a person with an appetite, metabolism, and levels of fat tissue that are regulated normally.

Evidently, it does not take much to knock these signaling systems out of balance. Obesity, diabetes, and overeating disorders are at record levels.

Stress, problems with work, romance, and family life, the experience of loss and grieving, as well as aging change our metabolisms and leave us vulnerable to craving more than we need. Humans did not evolve in environments with triple bacon cheeseburgers and Super Big Gulps easily available, and the presence of such energy-intense, calorie-rich stimuli in our modern settings triggers our minds to crave what very few of us need.

Chapter 5

Living With Binge Eating Disorder

❋ ❘ ❋ ❘ ❋ ❘ ❋ ❘ ❋ ❘ ❋ ❘ ❋ ❘ ❋ ❘ ❋ ❘ ❋ ❘ ❋ ❘ ❋ ❘ ❋

Binge eating is similar to other eating disorders in the sense that it comes with certain psychological issues that make things even worse. In this chapter, I'll be focused on certain traits exhibited by typical bingers. Identifying these traits is a major step to fixing the problem. Living in denial never really helped anyone, no?

1. **Enough disgust to fill a bucket:** The most popular word used by binge eaters to describe the feeling after an episode is 'disgust.' This emphasizes the feeling of shame that washes over them when they just finished downing three plates of noodles. The frequency of this feeling is solely dependent on the frequency of the episodes, and for the heavy bingers, they almost always feel this way. This feeling intensifies right after a seemingly good diet plan. I'll tell you why. Binge eaters go on a diet to give themselves a sense of control over their urges. They feel relieved and purified, but for a short while before everything comes

crashing down and they're back to the very feeling they managed to avoid for weeks, even months.

2. **The fear of never stopping:** You know that feeling of despair that fills your core when you feel stuck? Like there's no escaping your reality? That's the disorder messing with you. Once you think there's no way out, it further solidifies the hold bingeing has on you because you feel like there are no other options to deal with your problem except eating them away. You begin to rely on bingeing to handle problems that actually require real solutions. You are stuck because you are barking at the wrong tree to fix your problems like eating to deal with loss or dieting to deal with shame.

3. **Weight equals self-worth:** No matter how much you invest in delivering an outstanding performance or a stand-up character, at the end of the day, you won't feel worthy because you're not thin enough. You start to feel unworthy of attention and other things because you are ranking above the desired weight standard set by society. You might even think you will never be accepted until you shed a lot of pounds.

4. **You're a perfectionist:** If you're currently dealing with binge eating disorder, you're probably one of the most self-conscious people you know, but you'll never admit it. You set ridiculously high standards for yourself and tend only to pay attention to your mistakes than your amazing

achievements. The best way to phrase it is 'A person that demands perfection and no less from themselves yet never full of confidence that you won't fall short of your unreasonably high mark.' A few good examples of perfectionists in action include: Caroline is the project manager this year. She walks into the office, and everyone is clapping and showering her with praises for a project well done. However, she feels undeserving of all that because she's busy thinking of all the things she could have done if she had a little extra time. Another one is, Elizabeth is really stressed out over Dan's birthday tomorrow. She has absolutely no idea what gift to get him and this worries her because she takes pride in always having the perfect gift. She won't be able to stomach Dan's reaction to a less than perfect gift. This perfectionist personality doesn't just end at your eating habits; it slowly seeps into your everyday life and dealings.

5. **Everything is black and white:** This is pretty self-explanatory. It means arranging your thoughts and life experiences in a this-or-that manner with little or no space for anything else in between. This method of thinking is usually handed down in families from generation to generation. Families affect our thought processes more than we know. I'll give some black-and-white thought process examples: *"my work is amazing, or my work is downright horrible" "I stuck to my diet plan exactly as I wanted to or I messed up again" "I am a size 6, or I'm grossly overweight"*. This toxic method of viewing life is not just particular to

binge eating. It also affects people with bulimia and anorexia. This method of thinking is definitely setting you up for binge eating just out of desperation or feelings of guilt after a job 'horribly done' according to you. This trait doesn't just develop once you have BED; it is something you were already living with. Try gray areas, very shiny.

6. **Seeking approval from outsiders:** This particular behavior happens to plague everyone with an eating disorder. This means putting more faith in how others see you than your own opinions of yourself. Aiming to please is a very good example and changing yourself to suit the views and preferences of others just so they will like you. This pattern of thinking will definitely affect a lack of trust in your own compass and eventually crush your self-esteem so that you always look to others to make you feel good or validate your behavior. This behavior can stem from your family or friends, and at this point, you're probably wondering how this affects your binge eating habits. I'll tell you. Society has a way of conditioning people, especially people that feel the need to be conditioned. They tell you how you should look, talk and act and to secure a place in said society for validation's sake, you start to live up to their expectations, whatever this may be. There are two ways it can go, you can either diet and then relapse (binge), or you can diet, fail, feel depressed, or frustrated, then binge. Either way, seeking validation is booking you a first-class ticket to binge eating, especially if you already have the disorder.

Am I a Binge Eater?

The big question. The good thing is that I have a pretty straightforward questionnaire that can guide you to your discovery of whether or not you have BED. Just to put this out there, this is just a profiling method. It is not a substitute for a proper diagnosis by a health care professional, which I am not. So how to do this? Just count each question that feels mainly true, and when you get to the end, I'll explain the scoring system. Here goes:

1. I let my body size determine my self-worth most of the time.

2. When I binge, it almost feels like I am not myself at that moment. Like I am just watching myself shove food down my throat.

3. I am obsessed with weight, calorie counting, and food. I think about them all the time.

4. I am more likely to binge eat when I feel extremely bad, lonely, or simply overwhelmed.

5. I binge eat a lot (consuming insane amounts of food in a relatively short period of time.

6. I get this feeling of disgust, hopelessness, and worthless after an episode.

7. During a binge episode, it feels like I have zero control over my actions.

8. I've attempted every diet known to man, and I have done so strictly.

9. I can do anything to make sure people don't find out about my bingeing. It feels better as a secret.

10. It is pretty normal for me to start and quit diets so many times in a single year.

11. My weight fluctuates a lot within a short period

12. I either relapse on a diet or follow it as strictly as possible. There is no in-between.

13. Making the decision to begin another diet plan gives me a sense of control over my urges and hope for a thinner future.

14. I usually don't feel good enough about myself.

15. Every time I get to that point in my diet where I feel like I can't go on anymore because the rewards are obviously lesser than the effort.

16. I regularly find myself in a pit of depression.

17. I breathe validation.

18. I feel I would love myself more if I happened just to be thinner. I know others would.

19. I am a perfectionist deep in my bones. Dot all the Is and cross all the Ts.

20. I usually feel judged by people. It's almost like they always find fault in everything I do.

How to score: You get one point for every item you counted as mainly true about yourself. If you have 13 or maybe 12 points to your name, you should take it easy because you're showing a lot of red flags for binge eating disorder. You're hanging by a thin thread over the line between BED and just simple bingeing, but it'll be wise to pay more attention to curbing your red flags.

If you have over 15 points or exactly 15 points to your name, you're definitely a binge eater, and I'm doing this to scare you. It's more about creating awareness and treating the problem. It is not a virus, so it can be fixed. Just stick with me.

Different Ways Your Body Suffers as a Binge Eater

Binge eating might not be taken very seriously because you may think that the only effect it has is size fluctuations, but that's not all there is. Eating disorders, especially binge eating, have paved the way for a lot of very unpleasant, dangerous, and very painful side effects. Side effects like tooth enamel erosion or the growth of very soft downy hair on your arms called lanugo or something life-threatening like heart failure. Despite the surface effects, binge eating does a lot of serious damage to your body, way beyond what you can perceive and these damages are far from pretty. Take lanugo for example, it's a sure side effect 0f eating disorders and despite how shocking it is, it isn't exactly high on the dangerous scale. However, I can't say the same for others. These other effects are downright dangerous and life-threatening. Imagine your life being threatened by your somewhat purposeful eating habits not even a car or serial killer. The good thing is, a good number of the damage gets fixed while you're on treatment for the disorder. The other ones are not so treatable, rendering you impaired for life, and I bet you don't want to get to that point of no return, right?

If you're wondering why I'm telling you all these, it's because being aware is one of the major weapons you should have in your inventory. Any increase in awareness about the truth of BED, no matter how little, can go a long way in contributing to a speedy and steady recovery. Now we'll take a quick look at the dangers that accompany binge eating and the harmful effects on the human body. Eating disorders don't exactly come with labels or a manual, so your amour consists of your awareness and understanding of the problem and willingness to make better choices about your well-being. Let's look at the health risks:

- *Dehydration*

This puts you at a high risk for heart failure and much more. Remember, one of the major causes of bingeing is strict dieting. This starvation robs your body of way more than just nutrients gotten from solid food. You're also losing out on hydration. Water is essential for the body's daily functions. Every food you can think of contains some sort of liquid nourishment that can't be substituted for just water, and severely robbing yourself of the consumption of these nutrients and water can render the body dehydrated over some time. Starving yourself of good fats and carbs is also one of the causes of dehydration. You might wonder what makes hydration such a big deal. I'll tell you; hydration contributes to the increase in levels of certain minerals called electrolytes. It also impacts on heart function. Electrolytes are simple but important minerals like potassium, sodium, and calcium that can melt in liquids. Once they are completely dissolved, they have the electric charge of either positive or negative. This charge enables them to behave like transport vehicles moving materials into and out of body cells, whenever required. These minerals also carry electric impulses to muscle fibers to get them moving. Potassium and calcium are the minerals that specially handle one of the most important organs in the body, the heart. These electrolytes are responsible for inducing a normal and steady heartbeat. When there's an imbalance of electrolytes, one of the results can be a sudden heart attack, irreversible heart failure and even death. We all get dehydrated every once in a while and we should fix it as quickly as we can seeing as it is one of the early signs of cardiac arrest followed by an irregular heartbeat. If these symptoms are left unchecked, the following can happen:

- **Heart muscle atrophy:** In simple terms, this means that the muscles of your heart are wasting away. When your heart is weak, it won't beat properly, and if you deny your body the necessary nutrients it needs to repair itself, the problem will only get worse. The heart is not immune to starvation but gets affected just as much as any other organ. It needs some love too.

- **Low blood pressure:** This happens when your body is trying to use less energy to function. When you starve yourself, your body basically changes gear to battery saving mode, and this is dangerous.

- **Orthostatic hypotension:** Ever stood up too quickly and just felt this wave of dizziness? This happens when your blood pressure is low, and your heart is struggling to pump blood.

A lack of electrolytes even affects the efficiency of your nervous system to respond to stimuli. This is very manageable when you're fairly healthy, but it is dangerous when the heart is already weak. It can lead to a series of very unfortunate events seeing as your heart is the powerhouse that has been running since your birth. Anyway, enough about the heart, for now, there are other very harmful effects of dehydration (electrolyte imbalance) like liver failure or permanent damage, muscle weakness or immobility, kidney failure or permanent damage, seizures, convulsions etc.

Dehydration is particularly dangerous when type 1 or 2 diabetes is involved. Dehydration disrupts the blood sugar level, and too much sugar in your system can be very dangerous to some body tissues and can do a permanent number on certain organs like the kidneys and the eyes. Another issue concerning diabetes is the medications. A lot of the medications that keep people with diabetes alive have weight gain as a major side effect, and being a binger that deals with fat shaming, you will feel the need to cut back 9n your food consumption, and this comes with very life-threatening consequences.

I'm sure you probably see dehydration as a monster with a pitchfork and two horns, as you should, but there are some not-so-threatening effects of dehydration. They impact your quality of life, and nobody really likes living that way. I'll list a few nonlethal effects that you are already experiencing if you're dieting and a binge eater or should expect from strict calorie restriction.

1. Constipation

2. Bloated stomach

3. Presence of dark circles under the eyes.

4. Leg cramps

5. Fatigue/weakness

6. Headaches

7. The inability of your body to properly circulate blood during strenuous activities like exercises

8. Edema (This means swelling in the legs and feet)

9. Obviously dry skin

- ***Malnutrition***

First of all, this undermines your body's important systems. Denying the body of proper nutrition through purposeful starvation, you step into a state called malnourishment. Malnourishment is a result of lack of certain body essentials like fats, minerals, carbohydrates, vitamins, and fats. These minerals are basically consumed, and if you're not consuming anything or getting them artificially, you will become malnourished over time, and underneath the surface, a lot is going wrong with your basic human functions like:

- **You start missing menstrual periods (amenorrhea):** This happens because starvation isn't exactly an ideal condition for your body to produce the hormones that usually induce monthly menstruation. If you're not starving, another cause could be excessive exercise.

- **Fertility issues:** This should be obvious, but I'll spell it out. No period, no baby.

- **Loss of bone density (osteoporosis) or bone minerals (osteopenia):** This raises your chances of bone fracture from a two to ten as a result of certain deficiencies like calcium and estrogen. If it's not either of those things, your body is definitely producing a hormone called cortisol, also known as the stress hormone. Binge and purging only makes this worse.

- **Possible immune abnormalities:** Science has shown that a starved body doesn't contain quite a number of the body's immune cells, and these cells are essential for the prevention of a lot of infections, so you're putting yourself at risk of things I can't even name.

- **Multiple organ damage or failure:** You don't think ordinary starvation can do this? Try it and see if all the organs in your body don't pack up for the holidays.

- **Stunted growth:** When younger people still in the growth process fall into any eating disorder traps, this can restrict their growth and lead to the consequences of a lifetime.

- **Severe sensitivity to cold (cold feet and hands):** Thanks to starvation, your body temp regulator starts to act a bit wonky, and what's more when you don't eat properly, you lose fat, which is that nice layer of warmth you don't even know is there. Imagine its winter, will you throw your coat and gloves in the gutter? I think not!

- **Lanugo:** This is a condition where your body starts to grow down-like body hair. It happens because your body feels you're still worth redeeming from your bad decisions and is giving you a nice coat to warm up and think of a way to fix things. From the previous problem, I'm sure you can see why you need to warm up.

- **Easy and long-lasting bruising:** Everyone needs certain vitamins to heal from all injuries, even the ones as tiny as a papercut, and during starvation, your body is too busy trying to keep you alive by diverting energy to all the major organs and neglecting the production of these healing vitamins. When your blood pressure is low as well, you just entered the red zone.

- **Pale skin and anemia:** Anemia is a condition where you don't have as many red blood cells as your body needs to carry oxygen up and about to all the interested tissues. It is usually caused by iron deficiency, and one of the telltale signs is pale skin and eyes.

- **Hair, nails, and skin damage:** This happens when you lack vitamins. Your hair and skin start to dry up. Your hair breaks. Your let nails break. It's not pretty, I tell you.

Binge-Purge Cycle

Purging is a way of expelling unwanted goods from the body. Normally, the body does this all by itself to the bad guys as a way of maintaining balance and good health, but when you start to induce this action yourself, there's usually a problem. Some binge eaters purge to get rid of the 'excess' calories they consumed before the body starts the absorption process because of the guilt and shame of eating so much. Let's look at some purging methods:

- Using enemas

- Vomiting

- Using diuretics(i.e., products that induce and increase the urge the urinate also known as water pills)

- Using laxatives

Purging frequently makes you lose more water than you can replace, which even leads to dehydration, and you know what that's about. Purging also causes wear and tear of the body and a load of other harmful effects we'll be looking at right now:

- ***Depriving your body of fluids***

When you purge through whatever method you like, it's not just the food that comes up, a lot of water tags along and purging as frequently as you binge doesn't give a lot of room for as much rehydration as you will need unless you're a hundred percent sure you replace every drop of water you lose when you purge every single time. Losing water reduced the efficiency of your body functions. Another important thing purging robs you of is electrolytes, I mentioned them earlier if you remember. Anyway, when you purge, you create an imbalance of minerals, which can lead to cardiac arrest or slow heart rate. For more information on the heart and dehydration, scroll up to the previous topic, "Dehydration."

As always, awareness is very important when dealing with dehydration by purging. You need to understand exactly what you're up against. The first thing you should know is that you will be putting important organs in danger and this can have lasting consequences, maybe not as lasting as a starving person but I'm sure you won't be bothered about the difference when your health is at risk. Purging can do a number on you, even if it isn't lethal. Another thing to know is, if you're into the starvation and purging business, you have another thing coming because that is like beating yourself with a spiked baseball bat. Your body can handle water loss better if you're eating, at least, but if you're not, you'll be too weak to do anything about it.

- ***It causes wear and tear on the body***

Purging is a guaranteed way to cause major wear and tear on certain body parts. These painful and harmful side effects get worse depending on the frequency of purging, the amount of energy used to expel the food, and the amount of energy your body has left from dealing with other side effects of bingeing and purging. Let's take a look at the most bothersome wear and tear effects:

- **Puffy face:** The swelling of salivary glands causes this during vomiting.

- **Sore throat:** This damage to the throat is from the tools used to prompt vomiting. This also causes choking.

- **Damaged blood vessels in the eyes:** This happens when you strain to throw up.

- **Tooth enamel erosion:** You can damage your teeth when you frequently expose it to stomach acid every time you vomit.

- **Inflammation, ulceration, or rupture of the esophagus:** This is caused by vomiting and can require surgery as in a ruptured esophagus. A torn one leads to shock.

- **Reflux:** There is a muscle somewhere in between your stomach and esophagus that acts like a valve keeping the stomach acids in the stomach. When it gets damaged, the stomach acids can come up to play, and you wouldn't want heartburn or damage to your esophageal lining, would you?

- **Erosion, bleeding, or rupture of the stomach:** This can happen when you frequently strain to vomit.

- **Pancreatitis:** This simply means inflammation of the pancreas. When this happens, the pancreas gets swollen, your abdomen starts to hurt severely, and you get feverish.

- **Hiatal hernia:** This is a condition where a portion of the stomach pushes up into the chest cavity through the diaphragm. It happens when you frequently strain to vomit.

- **Chronic diarrhea:** When this happens, know that you have lost control over your bowel movements. This is due to the frequent use or abuse of laxatives.

Another important thing is the danger of ipecac syrup. This is usually used to prompt vomiting, but regular use can cause poisoning. This syrup is harmful to the muscles, and frequent usage causes a buildup of it in your system, which can result in cardiomyopathy, which, in simple terms, means wasting away of the muscle fibers of the heart. It can also cause shock, heart failure, coma and seizure. Just so we are on the same page about this, this syrup can kill you in a heartbeat.

Chapter 6

Binge Eating Midlife

D id you think binge eating only affected young people? The middle-aged population is coming out in droves to seek treatment, most especially middle-aged women. Many of them already dealt with eating problems in the past, much earlier in their life, and this is the second bout. Others are very new to this, having never experienced anything similar earlier in life. Something shocking is how many members of the senior generation (65 and older) go through major binge eating episodes and other eating problems. The numbers are more than a lot of health care professionals think.

Living in a culture that is absolutely obsessed with weight, age doesn't automatically make a person immune to these demands. The pressure to be thinner is so overwhelming that middle-aged and senior women fall victim to binge eating.

This chapter is dedicated to the pressures particular to the middle-aged and senior population and how binge eating seems like the brightest idea in their situation.

Weight Loss and Old Age

The activities of the older generation are not exactly high on the list of interesting things in our culture. In fact, the older you get, the less important or captivating you become. The young and beautiful people bingeing in secret and wasting away are the kind of things we'd rather pay attention to. For this reason, there hasn't been a lot of research conducted on binge eating among the middle-aged and seniors, so not a lot of people know just how badly binge eating has eaten into their generation. Taking a peek at some of the research that has actually been conducted on the subject, there are pieces of information that show links between binge eating and people over 30. They also show a rise in requests for treatment, rise in the rate of risk factors for their ages, and high mortality due to a number of reasons, some of which I have listed above when discussing the harmful effects of binge eating, especially the binge-purge cycle. This made me realize that no one is really too old to binge.

Losing the Fight for Youth and More

When you get to midlife, assuming you're not there yet, you'll realize that it is not a breeze or a walk in the park emotionally and practically. Somehow, it happens that society has found more interesting ways to stress middle-aged women then there's the extra stress that comes with aging, and now there's a spike in eating disorders among middle-aged women, how shocking. Certain special pressures can inch older people closer to binge eating.

Having a midlife crisis is no fun even though a lot of middle-aged men and women find satisfaction at that point in their lives for their life accomplishments. Imagine you're a 55-year-old engineer with a lovely wife, four kids, and a grandchild. You have worked so hard over the years, saved money, trained your children, made life-changing contributions to society, and you're about to retire from the hassle. You get to enjoy your pension and the sweet joy that comes with being around the people you love. It paints a nice picture, doesn't it? It should be a nice picture but not everyone has the same luxury, especially with the times. For a lot of people, this time becomes a period of overwhelming feelings of pressure, loss, being considered as less than worthwhile according to society. You won't be as beautiful or as energetic as you used to be, and the transition into this reality is a very difficult pill to swallow.

Introducing the "Sandwich Generation"

The people in midlife have been called the sandwich generation because, just like a sandwich, they are usually caught up in the middle of caring for their dependent kids and their equally dependent old parents. Now sprinkle a lot of financial responsibilities on this. Responsibilities like dealing with a mortgage, saving for college, health premiums for the whole family, and much more. Being middle-aged is more complicated than your teens because you might just be making real progress for the first time in your career or attempting to get back on the market after having a baby or you might be one of the many women who have their first child at 40 and you just made a dramatic entrance into the labor-intensive years. All I'm trying to point out is that there is no time in your life when you are going to feel like you're being pulled in a lot of directions at the same time, except college, I don't even know which is worse. In both cases, you have to somehow make it work

Loss Becomes the Most Felt Emotion

While dealing with all the demands that accompany being middle-aged, you'll experience more loss than any other time in your life. The resources or people that helped you get through certain things will no longer be there. Acceptance of these events can put your stress levels on a different kind of high and change your perception of yourself. Let's take a look at some of the losses people experience in midlife.

- **Death:** The first thing that may come to mind is the loss of your parents, and no matter how much you try to prepare for that, it won't hurt any less. However, another painful one is the loss of your friends to so many different circumstances, foreseen and unforeseen.

- **Getting divorced:** This one will rip your life apart, and it doesn't matter if you're the person who chose it or got stuck with the other person's choice. Either way, it hurts, and even though you'll eventually get back on track, you'll go through a period of confusion and loss. If you got stuck with it, you'd feel a lot more pain than the person who requested it. Statistics claim that most women's' standard of living takes a nosedive after a divorce.

- **Your kids will leave eventually:** One day, the nest will be empty. Your child leave for college or move out of the house or even get married to start families of their own, and this can be either relieving or painful. However, this point in life requires you to redefine yourself and what you're supposed to be doing with your life. That is a very difficult transition for some.

- **The youthful dreams of youth:** In midlife, you get a major reality check. You're not a vampire. You are going to leave this earth eventually, and time is running out. You have so much to do and achieve, and so little time. You might even be in a better position to pursue that dream career but there isn't enough time to make a mistake. You might need to accept the unfulfilled life you're currently living or take a chance on whatever new path you would like to take. Big decision.

- **Fertility:** Despite not wanting to have (any more) children, knowing that you can make you feel somewhat womanly. Transferring all that energy into something else requires a substantial amount of effort.

- **Physical strength:** Midlife is the time of acceptance. Know what else you will have to accept when you're middle-aged? The new limitations of your strength. You might not be able to go as long and hard as a 20-year-old at the gym anymore. That's a bummer.

- **Physical beauty:** Keep in mind that beauty is relative, and here, I am talking about beauty as defined by society. Some people have the luxury of aging beautifully; others do not. Besides, despite the number of compliments you receive from people about your 'beauty,' you may not feel as confident as you used to in your younger years because of your current perception of self, especially measured against society's current idea of beauty.

All these and more can reduce a person's self-esteem and predispose them to stress, frustration, and depression, which are the major causes of binge eating. Binge eating for the middle-aged is a way of escaping the justifiably stressful reality they live in. However, the cons outweigh the pros, and binge eating is more dangerous for the elderly because of their already failing body systems. Later in this book, effective treatment plans will be listed, so relax and read on.

Chapter 7

Binge Eating Disorder in Males

Ever seen a male with an eating disorder? I don't think so, but that doesn't mean they do not exist. Oh, they do, in large numbers. Sudden and extreme loss of weight in males is usually attributed to things like AIDS, depression, or even drug abuse. If a man purchases two medium-sized pizzas and downs them really quickly, it's usually regarded as normal since boys 'eat a lot'. It can't be that he's actually binge eating, right? These are only the tip of the iceberg concerning males and binge eating. This chapter is dedicated to educating people in the occurrence of binge eating in males, how to identify and understand it. We will also be reviewing the factors that predispose a male to binge eating disorder then I will point out certain issues that have to be considered when seeking treatment for males

Recognizing and Accepting that Guys go through Binge Eating Episodes

Many more men than we realize go through binge eating episodes. Statistics claim that over a million men living in America have binge eating disorder. The most recent study from the Medical

School of the University of Harvard proposes that at least 23 percent of adults living with binge eating disorder in the United States are male. Women are leading, however, in bulimia and anorexia as just about six to ten percent of bulimics and anorexics are men. In the world, men with binge eating disorder constitute about forty percent of the affected population; some studies even say that the numbers are way higher than that.

Binge eating disorders in males are on the rise and fast. The number of men seeking diagnosis and treatment is climbing, and this development has been noticeably going on for about a decade now. Another major thing that has come to light in the past decade is male public dissatisfaction with their physical appearance. A lot males happen not to like the way their body looks as opposed to what society claims it should look like. I'm sure you see where I'm heading with this. This whole appearance shindig is one of the major risk factors for binge eating disorder. The feeling of body dissatisfaction has always been associated with women, but men are opening up about the fact that they feel the same way sometimes. Certain studies designed to observe the culture and cultural shifts have claimed that there's a bridge developing between males and females, and this is because the pressure from society on males to look, act and talk a certain way has greatly increased. The female population has been conditioned to believe that they can achieve that perfect body through surgery, dieting, pills, exercise and others. Knowingly or unknowingly, men now think the same thanks to model images, adverts and magazine articles.

The Difference between Men and Women with Binge Eating Disorders

Speaking from a general point of view, binge eating in men is quite similar to binge eating in women. The signs, for instance, are very similar. Symptoms like having a warped body image, living with a fear of getting fat, having an unhealthy obsession with calories, and others are not particular to a single-gender. The same thing goes for the psychological behaviors the simmer underneath and fuels the problem. Behaviors like being obsessive-compulsive, believing that worth is equal to weight and body size, being a perfectionist, and others.

However, men and women change routes when deciding on the kind of changes they want in their bodies, how these changes will reflect their personality and the significance of all these to women. Most women aim for slimmer while most men look towards becoming bigger, buff. According to society, the ideal male has a body containing no fat, is shaped like a V, and has large biceps, which is an indicator of proper muscle distribution and the famous six-pack abs.

Most women are afraid of fat because they begin to feel unattractive. Most men are afraid of fat because they believe it makes them seem weak and soft. A good portion of the males dissatisfied with their physical appearance wants to gain some weight while the other portion wants to shed some. Either way, the aim for both groups is a bulky sculpted body. The use of steroids to achieve this goal of muscular perfection is another addition to the scary lengths men are willing to travel when motivated by any eating disorder, even binge eating.

There are other differences in how men and women perceive all major disorders (bulimia nervosa, anorexia nervosa, and binge eating disorder), and for knowledge sake, we'll breeze through the effects on men before getting back on the binge path.

- **Anorexia:** Starvation affects men very differently from women because of their biology. It reduces testosterone levels, which immediately kills the libido. In some, it does irreversible damage to their fertility. Irreversible meaning it can't be fixed even after weight restoration.

- **Bulimia:** Despite how unlikely (not impossible) it is for a man to purge, they usually lean towards other bulimic behaviors like calorie restriction or excessive and compulsive workouts

- **Binge eating disorder:** Men aren't as bothered as women about the behavior, and I highly think this is one of the reasons why their disorder goes unnoticed more than half of the time. Women experience shame due to binge eating, while men do not. Instead, they feel embarrassed when the effects of their behavior start to peek out through the fat on their bodies

Risk Factors for Males

Here we'll be taking a look at what predisposes men to binge eating disorder. Some of the risk factors we'll be looking at are similar to the ones found in the women's section, but others have 'only male' written all over it. While you're reading through, remember that the information here is not based on any definitive studies due to lack of research on the subject. However, these are the best assumptions of experts on the subject, so keep an open mind and read on.

- **Psychological factors:** Certain personality traits can make a person more likely to develop binge eating disorder, and these traits are similar to the ones found in the female section. They can also be called internal vulnerabilities. Some of these traits include:
  - Perfectionism
  - Need for external validation
  - Low self-esteem
  - Emotion management problems

- **Biographical factors:** Your upbringing and environment can have an effect on your mental development, and this can increase the risks of having BED. The distinctive risk factors under this umbrella are the same for both genders. They are:

  - **Family history:** Belonging to a certain family seems to raise the chances of developing binge eating disorder. Some families have very strict, almost choking lifestyles. They are overly organized and tightly bound by a lot of rules that cannot be broken without consequences. Other families are in dire need of structure. They are overly disorganized, and as a result, they cannot protect or support the family members as well as they should.

- ○ **History of trauma:** A lot of people with binge eating disorder has had some traumatic event happen to them in the past. This factor is not particular to any gender, as no one is immune to abuse or neglect. Some of these men endure sexual and physical abuse, loss of a loved one, and neglect because the parent of guardian remained nonchalant about their emotional and physical needs as a child. Another interesting thing that is particular to men is obesity during childhood. Some men with binge eating disorder have reported to have been overweight in their early years and this gave rise to teasing bullying, being used as a scapegoat, or even neglected because of their size. All these cause shame that extends into adulthood. This kind of body shaming may be more of a 'woman' thing but men get affected too.

- **Body dissatisfaction:** Not liking your body of feeling very unsatisfied about any part of it increases the likelihood of you taking corrective measures. Men with low self-esteem feel the burning need to be perfect for raising their self-esteem and be liked by others. This physical self-hatred can be a very dangerous weapon which leads men into binge eating disorder as a means to cope or fix 'the problem.' Men partake in similar binge eating behaviors that are dangerous to health. The only difference between what they do is the weight gain on the side of the men. Males are constantly subjected to pressure by the media to look a certain way to be appealing, and the higher thus gets, the more physically dissatisfied men we'll be seeing. In my opinion, healthy and acceptable weight should be based on body mass index (BMI) and not standards of people who may 0r may not care about you or your health.

- **Strict dieting:** Going on strict dieting or engaging in calorie restriction is another major risk factor. Dieting due to body dissatisfaction is something men and women go through. Despite the heat of physical perfection being mostly on women, men are starting to get burned regularly. Certain categories of men like the athletes or obese feel the pressure even more so you see members of those categories signing up to strict diet plans, which increases their risks of binge eating.

- **Shedding for sports:** Certain male sports activities that require a thinner build are perfect avenues for the development of the binge-purge cycle. Such activities include running, gymnastics, wrestling, swimming, being a horse rider, and others. I'll paint a quick picture. A regular healthy male athlete who has never had binge eating disorder or any disorder in his life decides to go on a diet to shed some pounds and maintain a specific weight. It starts out great, and he decides to continue to maintain the results. Dieting becomes a necessary aspect of his life, he does excessive workouts even to the point of physical harm and over time, and it gets more difficult because the hunger is starting to get to him. His body is requesting more food than he is willing to eat, then one day, he breaks and eats a whole lot of food uncontrollably. It's like his body took the reins for a minute, and when he's done, he proceeds to purge to rid himself of the excess calories because he shouldn't have eaten so much. Anything to keep his weight in check.

- **Being homosexual:** Certain experts have estimated the number of gay people with binge eating disorder to be 20% of the affected population. However, they are not sure if the basic features of being homosexual influence these numbers. There's a lot of speculation that the desire for gay men to constantly look appealing raises their risks 0f binge eating disorder. Definitive studies, however, have proven that the pressure on gay men to reach the ideal body goal is only a close second to the pressure that western heterosexual women go through.

How Men Escape BED Diagnosis

Most men deal with their eating disorders on their own for a long time before anyone even notices the signs. This is partially because of ignorance on the subject and partially because of secrecy. This is a serious problem because the longer a person has binge eating disorder, the more difficult it is to fix. If treatment is delayed, the chances of permanent damage increases (Check chapter 5 for more information). It is much easier for men with binge eating disorder to go completely unnoticed because a lot of people, including the affected men, aren't aware of the possibility of a man being a binge eater. The male binge eaters and the people close to them are not exactly on the lookout for signs and symptoms of BED. You hardly find things you're not actively seeking out. This lack of awareness affects every level where the disorder can be identified, beginning with the affected man. Let's take a look at these levels.

- **The man with the disorder:** So far, men have not been educated or exposed to the methods of prevention like the women. The media doesn't exactly parade affected male celebrities as a means of awareness. If a man is a binge eater, denial is most definitely part of his daily routine. A male binger would go through a long list of other reasons for his uncontrollable urges before he finally settles on binge eating, and even that is dependent on his knowledge of its existence. Let's say he happens to know what it is; he is more likely to dismiss it as a male thing. Men who go through the binge-purge cycle do so in less obvious ways than women. They are likely to lean on excessive exercises. The whole point is that a lot of men are clueless about their disorders, and it can easily stay this way for a long time.

- **Family and friends:** These are the ones who motivate females they care about to identify their disorder and get help. This is partially because it is generally believed to be a female thing, so people are naturally on the lookout and partially because women are more open about things like this. Men, on the other hand, are not one to talk about their weight and eating habits with friends and family.

- **Health care professionals:** Some research has revealed that medical professionals find it easier to link obvious symptoms like weight loss to other issues, not binge eating. They'll usually go through depression, AIDS, and drug abuse first because they seem like a plausible explanation for male weight loss.

I am honestly not trying to label anyone as nonchalant or negligent. I am just putting the fact that males binge eating disorder isn't as loud as the female one out there. It hasn't exactly made it to the news yet, but it is a real thing. I mean, as a man, you're unlikely to accuse a binge eating disorder of being the cause of your bad eating habits even when the signs are crystal clear.

There's another good reason why so many male binge eaters go unnoticed and untreated. This reason is that they are not so excited about stepping forward to admit they actually do have a problem, especially when they realize what the problem is. Eating disorders, in general, have been said to be a woman's problem, so men fear they would be emasculated, ridiculed, or even seen as weak if they admit to having a 'woman's problem.' These fears just add to the feelings of shame and the need for secrecy.

Being Male in a Treatment World Wired for Females.

As a man with binge eating disorder, if you eventually manage to recognize your issue, shove the shame in a Ziploc bag and take the necessary steps needed to get treatment, you willingly waltz into a world wired for females. This world doesn't have any program limitations. The partial hospital program, support group program, an intensive outpatient program, or even group therapy are deeply affected, so much so that some of them are a females-only program. In the ones that manage to leave room for the men, ironically, they're sure to not be at the top of the priority list. This automatically means that by numbers and plain tradition, the females will get a lot of time to talk about binge eating from their perspective which is really an important part of the treatment plan. Men, however, don't get to speak very often and as a result, the need to share, understand and be understood is crushed. These female-dominated groups almost always have the males feeling like they do not belong. Some people have claimed that this shouldn't be an issue since the symptoms and experiences are very similar for both genders but I think that opening up, talking, and being understood is a vital part of recovery for both genders, and males should be allowed in on the juice.

Some others have argued that a man living with binge eating disorder must understand that issues like sexuality, body image, and certain others are gender-specific and should be discussed in a group of strictly male participants. This argument doesn't really serve anyone seeing as there are no groups like that in existence yet. The aim, however, is to create a certain awareness of binge eating disorder in men so that more services will be directed to diagnosing and treating them.

Chapter 8

Mindfulness

Mindfulness simply means purposely directing your attention to the present accompanied by qualities like curiosity, acceptance, and compassion. When you practice mindfulness, you learn to live in the moment while actually enjoying your experience instead of being bothered about the past or future. The past no longer exists, it has happened, and there's really nothing you can do but dwell on it. The future is totally a mystery and clearly isn't here yet. The present, however, is right here, and you have only now to truly live it up.

Mindfulness basically teaches you how to experience this moment and every single thing that comes with it. This is the way to make the most of right now (the only time you have to make decisions, smile, create, think, live, listen or act) and turning it into the most fulfilling experiences of a lifetime. You can learn and practice mindfulness through regular meditation for as many minutes or hours as you'd like. This chapter is just an introduction to mindfulness, and in a few, we will be discussing mindfulness in relation to binge eating. I'm sure you can already see the connection but if you can't, you will soon. Stick with me.

Understanding the Meaning of Mindfulness

The practice of mindfulness was originally created in ancient days and are mostly practiced by people of the western and eastern culture. The word 'mindfulness' is an English translation of Sati, an ancient Indian word which means awareness, remembering, and attention. Let's breeze through these words:

- **Awareness:** This aspect of mindfulness ensures you conscious and actively existing in your immediate environment. Awareness makes you notice everything around you; it is literally the act of being aware.

- **Remembering:** This one tells you to remember to observe every moment until the experience is over actively. A mindful person is quick to forget. Remember is an English translation of the *rememorari*, a Latin word that means to be mindful again.

- **Attention:** This is simply awareness that is directed at a particular object, person, or feeling. Mindfulness will teach you to make better decisions about where to invest your attention and how to sustain it.

Assuming you want to engage in mindful behaviors as a way of coping with stress. While you're at work, you're overwhelmed with thoughts about a presentation you're preparing for, and these thoughts begin to cause you more stress and anxiety. Once you become aware of this situation, you need to remind yourself to direct your attention to your breathing and keep it there instead of letting your mind run through all the possible ways the presentation could go wrong. Focusing on your breathing with a gentleness and a certain stillness will help calm you slowly but surely.

The man who directed mindful towards a more therapeutic route, Doctor Jon Kabat-Zinn said that mindfulness is a habit that can be developed through directing your attention here and now in a particular way that is completely unreactive, lacking judgment and openhearted. Let us breeze through the meaning of these things:

- **Here and now:** The reality of truly living in the present moment means that you need to observe the nature of things as they exist or are happening right now. Experiences are relative and should be unique.

- **Directing attention:** There is no mindfulness without paying attention to whatever you decide to pay attention to.

- **Unreactive response:** There's usually an immediate response to external stimuli, no matter what it is. This auto-response is a result of the previous condition by society, family, and friends. A good example is when you think you still have so much work to do, you automatically react a certain way to the feeling that accompanies that thought. Mindfulness is more about responding to your experiences than automatically reacting to your thoughts. No, they are not the same thing. A response is carefully thought out and deliberate, a reaction doesn't really leave a lot of room for thought.

- **Lack of judgment:** Sometimes, it feels almost impossible not to judge a thing, whether it's bad or good. There is a different kind of bliss that comes with discarding judgment. This will help you perceive things for what they truly are instead of putting them through a judgment filter based on past experiences and external influence.

- **Openhearted:** Mindfulness concerns the heart as much as it concerns the mind. Being openhearted is to be kind, warm, compassionate, and friendly, too, while having your experience. A good example is noticing that you think you're useless at trying to meditate, then you nicely accept that this thought flew through your head before you let it go and calmly return your focus to meditation.

Looking at Mindful Meditation

Mindful meditation is a specific type of meditation that has been tested and well-studied, even in clinical settings. This kind of meditation isn't about the absence of thoughts in your mind. Instead, it is the act of directing attention to a particular object, movement, feeling, thought, or sound. You can even focus on the awareness of your own thoughts and by listening to them, you get to map out certain patterns like a loop. Anything that goes through your mind at any given time has more effect on how you feel than you realize so awareness is very helpful when it comes to dealing with said feelings. During mindful meditation, you can choose to focus on one or more of the following:

- Any of your five senses.

- Your thoughts or feelings

- The feeling of your breathing

- Whatever you're most aware of at the time

Mindful meditation has two distinct branches. Let's check them out:

- **Formal meditation:** This is the kind of meditation you plan for. You intentionally make out time to be still and meditate. Making this decision allows you to prepare to deepen your meditation and understand more about your thoughts and feelings. It also teaches you to be mindful for longer than you're used to with a touch of kindness and curiosity directed at your experience and yourself. This meditation is a form of mind training.

- **Informal meditation:** This can happen at any point during the day. This kind of meditation means slipping into the meditative state going about your day and performing your usual activities like cleaning, eating, driving, cooking, having a conversation, etc. As you do this, you get better and better at mindfulness while training your mind to remain in the present and avoid swing back and forth between the past and the future. Practicing this kind of meditation teaches you to remain calm while being mindfully aware of what you're doing at any time during the day.

Practicing meditation doesn't mean doing rehearsals. It means engaging in the act of meditation as often as you can. Some people do this intending to perfect the art of meditation one day, which is really a wrong way to go about this. There is absolutely no need to put your meditation under the microscope. It is simply an experience, your experience. Mindfulness is a useful tool, especially with regards to binge eating, because they are absolute opposites. Mindfulness can be used in different areas of life, like walking, working, eating, cooking, etc. Mindfully meditating as a binge eater will help you focus more on the reason behind the urge rather than the urge itself. Or you could always eat mindfully. Let's see what that's about.

What Is Mindful Eating?

Remember having the habit of coming home in the evening and dropping on the couch to watch a movie with an insanely large bowl of chips of popcorn? You would literally mindlessly chew on the contents of the bowl until you reach inside to find nothing left, and you're just halfway through the movie. You ate them all.

What I would do is go get more, partly because I would honestly like more chips while seeing a movie and partly because I plan to savor the taste and enjoy each bite this time because that is what mindful eating is all about. This includes acknowledging the feel of each chip on my finger when I pick it up and then recognizing and savoring the salty taste when I place it on my tongue. It still entails awareness of the loud sound each bite makes as I chew away and the sound it makes in my head. While I mindfully eat the chips, I register their exact consistency against my tongue and the feeling of my teeth moving against each other. I feel my saliva wetting the chips as it proceeds to the back of my throat to slide down my esophagus. Mindful eating requires me to feel the food in my belly and awareness of the pleasure I received while eating it. During this watchful period, I notice the expansion of my stomach as it fills up from eating. I just experienced every single bite from the beginning till the end. I slowed down every section of the eating process to be totally aware of each of them and feel a certain connection to them.

That right, there is just a tiny example of mindful eating, and I'll do my best to drop lire along the way before the book is over. The point to focus on while you read is that this is a tested and surely effective way to reshape your eating habits and develop control over your mind and the way to go about this is recognizing and understanding your own thought patterns, your different appetites and emotional moods rather than having your old, impulsive and habitual thoughts to run the game. Eating mindfully is all about the following:

- Recognizing your hunger and fullness signs.

- Directing your attention to the whole eating process like being aware of the feel of the fork on your fingers.

- Having a certain awareness of how you eat.

- Choosing to truly taste the food by sensing and savoring it.

- Eating strictly for nourishment and exact hunger needs not because you had a bad day.

- Recognizing and understanding the feelings that make you want to eat (binge eat). These are your emotional triggers.

- Being consciously aware of your food choices.

- Developing a mindful and less judgmental mindset.

- Staying present and recognizing your appetite changes.

- Choosing to be observant and alert to your thoughts about food.

- Choosing to let go of critical thoughts

- Recognizing and accepting food for what it is and not putting some in the forbidden category.

- Calmly experiencing pre-eating and post-eating feelings.

- Showing compassion to yourself and others

- Accepting your body and your whole being as they truly are.

Mindless (binge) eating is categorized by the following:

- Choosing to eat because of emotional triggers instead of physical hunger.

- Having an eating or habitual routine.

- Multitasking while eating (Like driving, walking, talking, etc.)

- Grazing on food.

- Choosing to skip breakfast and other meals.

- The inability to stop eating despite feeling full.

- Choosing to ignore hunger and body cues like low energy or a rumbling tummy.

- Eating for comfort.

- Being an avid member of the clean plate club, i.e., you eat everything on your plate despite portion size.

- Living to eat rather than eating to live.

- Accepting that you have no control over your eating habits.

- Eating as if you're in a trance.

- Leaving room for the "I should" and "I shouldn't" to take over food consumption.

Shifting Out of Autopilot Eating

Sitting at the center of binge eating disorder is autopilot eating. I need you to take some time out to think about how it feels to be in a car on autopilot, then suddenly it screeches to a halt and wakes you up with a jolt. That's when you find out you zoned out throughout the ride. That right, there is the consciousness shift that takes place when you are pulled back down to reality after absentmindedly driving back home instead of the office. Your driving was impeccable, your hands turned the wheel when it should have, and your legs knew when to hit the brakes. However, you were just not there for any of it. This just reminds us how easy it really is to do even the most complicated things with zero thought or consciousness. Imagine how easy it would be to eat when you're on autopilot. Just hold your spoon and dig in, no need to be conscious so there'll be no thought involved. The bad thing is thoughts and actions that manage to escape your awareness still continue **without** your awareness and may end up taking you to places you don't want to go. Unhealthy behaviors find a way of persisting without your knowledge. For instance, you might automatically say "It's 1 p.m. and time to grab a snack" or whenever you're plopped on the couch at night ready to see a movie, you always have a bowl of pretzels by your side or you just find yourself automatically munching on a box of cookies every time you're stressed. These habits are almost reflexes. You do them so absentmindedly and effortlessly that it can be likened to brushing your teeth every morning or combing your hair, just things you do with little or zero thought.

If you happen to have a mindless eating habit or habits, they're going to remain exactly that, mindless, until you choose to shift awareness to them. When binge eating habits happen while you're conscious, you are in a position to think of effective ways to curb them. You can remember to find creative ways to let them go and form healthy eating habits.

To Be Mindful

Right now, while reading, you're getting your very first feel of mindfulness, but you truly absorb and understand these words; you need to shift from auto mode and pay attention to the words you're looking at right now. Mindfulness involves not only your eyes but all of your senses. You should also be aware and take note of your reactions while you read. Another important thing to do is accept everything you're looking at right now without judgment. That doesn't mean you believe them or will practice them; you just choose not to judge them. I would like you to keep these aspects of mindful eating in mind while you read:

- **Awareness:** Become attuned to your senses. Notice things, smell them, look at them, touch, and taste them.

- **Observation:** I need to view yourself as if you're an outsider looking in. It should feel like you're observing your actions in a movie. Take note of how you eat. Do you eat quickly? Slowly? Do you take big or small bites?

- **Existing in the moment:** Living in the present while you eat is more important than people realize. When you're eating, focus on just that. Don't be bothered by the future or the past because you can't do anything about them. You can only influence what you're eating right this minute.

- **Let go:** I need you to choose to not hold on to your emotional triggers, i.e., the thoughts and emotions that push you to eat. Learning to not respond to an urge is very important. Instead of a response, you let it go.

- **Being mindful of your environment:** I need you to take a good look around you, don't just glance. Do you see any of your triggers? Maybe you get triggered when food is within reach? Is there a commercial that makes you just want to munch on something? Is there an object that brings you bad memories that you need to quiet down with food? You need to be aware of these things.

- **Zero judgment:** Take all that criticism, guilt and shame then shove it violently in the trash. Instead of those emotions, talk kindly to yourself, feel compassion for yourself. This helps with self-honesty about your urges and the amount of food you eat. Don't judge yourself, just observe.

- **Acceptance:** Take things as they are. Stop trying to alter your physical appearance in any way to suit others. Rather, pay attention to your body.

Using Mindfulness to Help You

I'm sure you know what it feels like to be lost in thought. Normally, as you go through the day and its activities, your mind is free to wander where it may. This is you functioning on autopilot, and some of these thoughts might be harmless but the others, not so much. Some of these thoughts can be downright dangerous and, even worse, habitual. Sometimes, you can get so lost in these thoughts that you miss even the little things happening around you.

A good example is, say you're going for a nice walk in the park but you're thinking about your next project. Your legs are moving but your mind is completely occupied with the thoughts you're currently having. First thing to note is, you're not conscious of your environment. Another thing is that you're stressing yourself with those unhelpful thoughts. You're causing yourself anxiety and depression. If you're already a binge eater, the first thing that comes to your head is too much on something, anything at all, to get your mind off of your current emotions. However, if you practice or choose to practice mindfulness, you won't fix the thought (the project); instead you'll accept the emotions coming from that thought and choose to let them go. The first step to being mindful is acceptance; change will naturally follow. If you deal with anxiety issues, rather than living in denial or dwelling in the feeling, you accept it, and eventually, change will come. According to an old saying, what we try to resist will try to persist. Mindfulness teaches you to understand that what you accept will be transformed. Just so you don't get it twisted, acceptance has nothing to do with giving up or resignation. Instead, it is all about acknowledgment.

Acknowledging your binge eating disorder. Acknowledging your emotional triggers.

Allowing Space to Heal

This is for the seniors or anyone going through any kind of physical pain or impairment. Physical illnesses can be very depressing, especially one that has stood the test of time. Your illness might be lethal, extremely painful or both. Your problem may be affecting the quality of your life. Maybe you're not able to do even the simplest things like getting up to pee or move about freely. Illnesses like this can affect the very core of your existence and depression might result.

People are more likely to develop unhealthy coping mechanisms like binge eating. This might seem justifiable because one would claim to need to draw strength from anywhere possible to keep from drowning in despair and losing hope. Increased levels of stress over time have shown clear effects on the immune system, and it definitely doesn't strengthen it. Have you ever come down with the flu after a long period of intense stress? It seems unreal, doesn't it?

Studies have been conducted on caregivers who have been stressed for long periods of time, and it was discovered that they had weak immune systems and therefore were more susceptible to certain infections than their healthy colleagues. Mindfulness is an effective method of dealing with illnesses, and as a result, stress levels go down. This will give your immune system the needed jolt and might even speed up recovery assuming the illness isn't lifelong but even then, you'll noticeably feel better about yourself. Mindfulness has been established to be a pain, depression and stress reliever. It has been reported to reduce anxiety, boost creativity and strength of relationships. It is also known to increase energy levels and positively affect your self-image. The more you are mindful of your thoughts and actions, the easier it will be for you to finally be in control of your urges like you've always wanted

Chapter 9

Reaping the Benefits
of Mindful Eating

❀ I ❀ I ❀ I ❀ I ❀ I ❀ I ❀ I ❀ I ❀ I ❀ I ❀ I ❀ I ❀

This chapter is especially dedicated to understanding the effects of mindful eating on your life and emotions in general. Here we will explore the core of mindful eating. The pleasure derived from mindful eating is somewhat like the kind you get from dancing. Do you dance because you know and understand the cardiovascular and muscular benefits or for brain exercising from mastering complicated dance moves? Not exactly, you dance because it feels good, it makes you feel alive. Dancing with a specific goal in mind, kind of ruins the fun, don't you think? Dancing for dancing sake is pleasurable in itself, but then dancing for the fun of it doesn't remove all the health benefits from the equation, does it? Nope, that's just the cherry on top.

The same thing goes for mindful eating. Eating mindfully should be done for mindfulness sake. It should be all about establishing that connection with all your senses. It should be about curiosity and surfing through the waves of your mind. If you're overly focused on enjoying the benefits of mindful eating, you take all the fun out of it. The whole point of meditation isn't to reach a particular goal or destination. The destination is the journey, and that is what matters. Remember this while you go through the different amazing benefits of mindful eating below and allow the dance of mindful eating flow deep into your core. Relaxation, strengthened relationships with others, love of self and many others are just the cherry on top. The whole cake is everything else. Now let's look at a few cherries, shall we?

Deep Physical Relaxation

The physical body and the mind are almost one and the same. If you have anxiety running through your thoughts, your body taps into that emotion almost automatically. One cannot fully exist without the other. Do you ever wonder why our bodies tense up whenever we experience really high-stress levels? I'll tell you. This reaction is mechanically wired to our bodies. When we go through stressful situations, a full-blown chain reaction begins, and our bodies are kicked into the fight or flight mode. All this energy goes through our bodies and our bodies are almost always clueless as to what to do with all this energy so it quickly tenses up or in your case, starts to binge eat.

The purpose of mindful eating is not to get you to relax per se because relaxation just brings about more tension. Mindful eating goes farther than that. It is about being mindfully aware and choosing to accept the moments of urges as they come. This means that tension requires you to mindfully aware of that emotion, to acknowledge it. Where exactly, do you feel tense? Is it a body part or a mental feeling? If it's physical, what is the texture, shape and color of the part? How do you react to this feeling? How can you redirect this emotion? You see, mindfulness makes you genuinely curious about whatever you are experiencing. Now you can start breathing into the origin of the tension, taking kindness, acknowledgment and compassion with it. You shouldn't try to change or fight the tension; it'll only make it worse. That's all. Practicing this regularly will definitely relax you and help you better deal with your emotional triggers.

Getting Back in Touch

Babies are generally more in touch with their bodies than we are. They notice and feel even the subtlest sensations. They genuinely enjoy exploring and experiencing their immediate environment. However, growth slowly takes that away. You're no longer a baby, and I know for a fact that you now use your head more than your body. You're probably not as attuned to your body now as you were when you were still in your developmental stages. You also no longer take note of the subtle hints your body tries to give you through your mind. A lot of people think that the body is simply a tool used to carry the brain around, but what they probably don't know us that the communication better your body and mind is like a two-way street. It goes back and forth. They share information, sensations and so on. They are in constant communication whether you like it or not so the first thing to do here is being aware of this. For example, you think you like a particular drink, your body responds positively to this because when you drink it, the receptors in your tongue transmit a pleasurable feeling to your brain. This also happens when you feel like you need to eat, your body proceeds to satisfy that craving. What about emotions? When your shoulders tense up or your heart starts to beat really fast, your mind and body already had a conversation about a particular emotion or group of emotions. Your body just physically expresses it.

What happens when your mind is too busy to read the text messages from your body? Its phone has been buzzing for minutes, and it doesn't even notice. Whenever this happens, it means that the connection has been lost, and you aren't aware of your internal and external environment anymore. Tiredness, hunger, stress and thirst are clear instinctual signals that your mind can longer receive. This disconnection will only get worse if you don't choose to do something about it. This why some people find themselves bingeing uncontrollably until they are somewhat jolted back to reality. To avoid this, you should practice a mindful technique called the body scan. This entails you spend roughly 35 minutes or more moving your attention from one part of your body to the next. You start from the top of your head to the tips of your toes. For some, it feels like they are experiencing their body for the first time and it prompts them to want to pay more attention to their physical self. The body scan might seem like a lot at first if this is your first experience. This is the journey of a lifetime. You will feel a lot of things like feelings from your past that you buried in a forty feet hole for different reasons or emotions that you suppressed over time, trapped physical pain etc. So many times, people experience pain or a certain illness for a long period without an obvious cause. Meditation and mindfulness can help unravel the emotions you've suppressed over the years which automatically releases the emotion.

Final Stop! **Binge Eating**

Your body needs to be one with your mind to better understanding and properly handle emotions.

Boosting your Immune System

Whenever there's a problem with your body, it's usually the work of your immune system to deal with it. If your immune system is top-notch, you'll always be in the clear, but when your immune system isn't at its best, you're prone to a lot of health problems. Stress, among other things, can weaken the immune system. You know another thing stress does, it leaves you prone to unhealthy coping mechanisms but that isn't what this is about. This is about mindfully expelling stress to improve your immune system with is considered an all-round win but it is particularly important for binge eaters dealing with health problems that arose as a result of the disorder. You see, when your body system is threatened, it directed all the resources to deal with the threat and in the process, other functions are put on standby. Functions like your immunity. Stress isn't always a bad thing, ironically speaking. When your stress levels are dangerously low, you begin to lack a sense of motivation and everything automatically bores you. However, if your stress levels are dangerously high for a long period, your immunity is going to get benched until you deal with your triggers. Mindful behaviors teach you to be in touch and notice even the subtlest changes that occur in your body. How you can do this is by being mindfully aware of the situation and then think of healthy ways to expel it instead of depending on binge eating or some other unhealthy coping mechanisms. This way, it's 1 point for you and 0 for BED.

Reducing Pain

Discovering this shocked me too, but mindful behavior has been tested and trusted to reduce pain in participants that have been actively engaged for about eight weeks. I know a few people who have dealt with pain for a long time until they started practicing various mindful behaviors and meditation. Pain is an unpleasant feeling that we instinctively attempt to block out whenever it hits. You know how you accidentally hit your arm on the door and then automatically tighten the muscles around that area in a bid to reduce the pain or at least distract yourself until it goes away, that is one method people use to deal with pain. Another method is violence. You want the pain to stop so badly that you react violently. This only gives room for more pain and tension in every area of your body not just the affected portion. Sometimes it feels much easier to fight the pain but this only creates a barrier between you and what you feel and you may not know it but you're expending energy to deal with it. Or maybe you'd end up resigning to the feeling and end up drowning in helplessness. This reaction usually leads to binge eating which doesn't even give you lasting pleasure because the feeling comes right back when you're done eating.

Mindful behavior will take a whole different route to an even better result. When being mindful, you are required to direct attention to the pain for as long as you can. If it's your arm, instead of finding a distraction or reacting violently, you will pay attention to the area that hurts. You need to be mindfully aware of the sensations going through that area at the time, and you need to do so with curiosity, acknowledgment and kindness. This isn't magic and it permanently erase your pain with a single try but with regular practice, you will begin to see that you have developed a healthy coping mechanism. After a while, you can begin to take more of the differences between physical pain and the extra emotions you unconsciously throw in the mix. The difference between psychological and physical pain becomes clearer. Physical pain feels raw; it is that prick, burn, or bite you feel. On the other hand, psychological pain feels a lot like anxiety, loss, frustration and stress. Your mind translates physical pain into psychological pain and that doesn't feel Christmas, does it?

When you practice mindfulness even while eating, you slowly expel the psychological pain so that the only pain left is physical. As the psychological pain slowly dissolves, you should begin to feel the physical pain disappear. This is only possible if you change your perception of pain and acknowledge your reality, not run from it.

Calm your Mind

Remember when I said the purpose of mindfulness isn't for relaxation, but it happens as an added bonus? Well, the same thing goes for this. The purpose of mindfulness is not to bring calmness to mind but it is an added bonus. Think of the mind like an ocean. An ocean is wild on some days and calm on others. On some days, your mind keeps running from one thought to another without stopping to take a breather. On other days, your mind slows down a bit and you manage to have some space in between thoughts. Being mindful isn't particularly about changing the rate at which you think, it is more about being aware of the thoughts as they fly past.

This method helps you to take a few steps back from the hustle and bustle of your thoughts. By doing this, you stay above them and aware. The thoughts do not disappear but now you have the upper hand because of the awareness of the thought or emotion. Think of it like watching a movie instead of starring and being thrown around by the director. This way you choose which thoughts to respond to and which ones to let go of. This is like carrying a shiny armor to the binge fight. You are less likely to be triggered because you're in control.

Listening to your Thoughts

If you take time to look around you, you'll notice a lot of man-made objects unless you live in the river, which would be great because I'll be honored. Anyway, all man-made objects were only a thought once upon a time. A lot of people around the world believe in the power of thought. Every single word you utter, every action you perform, all the activities you indulge in are all products of your thoughts. This means that being mindfully aware of all your thoughts automatically makes you aware of your actions, which makes it easier to resist the urge to binge. It's usually effortless to get the brain to follow habitual patterns because when you think, the thoughts take a particular route. Every time a particular thought goes through your head or you do a particular thing, there's a high chance of you repeating it, and this way, you strengthen the connection between the neurons involved. Think of it as a workout. This is why binge eating is likely to recur after the first time, and the more you engage in binge eating, the harder it becomes to treat. A lack of mindfulness in these actions or thoughts can encourage the development of negative and unhelpful behaviors like body dissatisfaction that will persist if not nipped in the bud. This negativity begins to seep into every aspect of your life without your knowledge and it becomes a vicious cycle that you can't seem to escape. Mindfulness sort of opens your ears to your thoughts to better filter the positive from the negative.

Making Better Decisions

Decision making is a process we all go through every day, whether we know it or not. You chose to stick around until you got to this chapter. Soon, you'll choose to stop and get started on something different. Good decisions have a significant impact on your eating habits. All the binge eating episodes you have had are a result of choice. Choosing to binge eat, choosing to be affected by negative emotions, choosing your kind of coping mechanism and so on. Being mindfully aware of your physical body can assist you in making better decisions. You know that feeling you get in your gut about something? Scientists have proved that signal to be more accurate than actual logic. Studies have discovered that there is a bundle of nerves in the gut that resembles the kind found in the brain. This has been mostly used by top company CEOs in major decision making. Say Michael Eisner for example, the CEO of Walt Disney, said that until 2005, his body responded whenever he heard a great idea. He said he'd feel it in his throat, stomach, and even his skin. As a binge eater, it is almost as if you are wired to ignore this feeling, as you'd rather stay disconnected. Your conscious mind cannot handle the amount of information contained in your subconscious mind. Practicing mindful behavior enables you to tap into that huge memory box; it helps you to be more intuitive, more aware of the subconscious. This way, you can better control your 'controllable' urges because you are constantly in sync with your mind and body.

Coming to your Senses

A major key in all kinds of mindful behavior, even mindful eating, is the art of being calm. This calmness connects you to all your senses (smell, sound, taste, sight and touch). Have you ever heard any of these expressions?

- "That sounds sensible."

- "I sense a major problem."

- "She will soon come to her senses."

I'm sure you have. The popular use of "sense" tells us that people appreciate and attach value to being connected with all our senses. If you want to make a plausible decision, you automatically know the importance of being in sync with your senses while you do so. You wonder how choosing to connect with your senses will help your binge eating disorder? You should know that if you are not being focused on the information coming through all your organs of perception, you're just listening to your thoughts and feelings. You're completely unaware of anything else. You see, thoughts are products of past experiences, memories and yes, you are able to think up something new, but in general, your mind is wired around past experiences or future possibilities that depend on past experiences.

Another thing your thoughts influence is your emotions so whenever you choose to be unaware, you become lost in thoughts and memories, both pleasant and unpleasant. This can trigger unwanted behavior that will be acted out on autopilot. Connecting and staying connected to one or all 9f your senses, you automatically calm yourself a bit. When the thought starts to flood and the urges start to kick in, you can decide to mindfully focus on the sound of your breathing or the movement of your body as air enters and leaves. By choosing to direct your attention towards one of your senses, you keep your mind from wandering off to places it shouldn't go. You keep your triggers at bay. This is as mental as it is physical. You are training your mind to focus. While practicing this mindful behavior, your mind will stray sometimes but you don't have to feel disappointed or frustrated. All you need to do is gently redirect your focus. A quick rundown of the benefits of this particular mindful behavior:

- It trains your attention to focus.

- It helps you understand that you can choose to shift your attention towards your senses of perception, not your thoughts.

- You learn to be kind to yourself every time you get distracted.

- It helps you realize the amount of power you hold over deciding what you pay attention to.

- It helps calm your mind.

Preparing Yourself for Mindfulness

When deciding to practice mindful eating or any mindful behavior, you need to let go of any negative attitude you may have towards it. It's like starting an all-natural skincare routine and thinking, "this might not help. I don't think it'll work." Let's say you begin to have breakouts a week in; in your head, this only proved your point about it was not working and you give up immediately. Instead of all that negative energy, you should harbor a positive long-term vision for whatever mindful behavior you choose to practice. Don't think too much about it, don't wonder how long it will take to work, just know and trust that it will. Attempting the mindful eating practice is going to be rocky at first because the whole point of a binge is to wolf it all down but this, this will feel like you're eating in slow motion. It teaches you to really be present, appreciate and truly enjoy your meals. This practice is being upheld by millions of people across the world and backed up by countless studies. Mindful eating and mindfulness as a whole go hand in hand because mindful eating helps curb your feeding excess but they are bound to recur if you do not deal with th3 underlying problem, which is the emotional trigger. During my time teaching people about mindful behaviors, I have realized that being skeptical, not negative about it, works wonderfully. A good example is you having doubts about the practice but still trying it and sticking to it for a while and eventually realizing it works.

Looking Beyond Problem-Solving

Mindful eating shouldn't be regarded as a quick fix. It should be practiced on the days when you think you have it all under control and the days where you feel like you're right on the edge of losing it. Mindful behavior, in general, should be cultivated at your own pace but steadily and daily so that whenever things get rocky, you can always remember to mindfully focus on your breathing to quieten the noise in your head. Think of steady practice like using a helmet when riding a bike. You put the helmet on each time you hit the road, just to protect yourself in case you get into an accident. Nobody puts on a helmet right before an accident because you might honestly not remember because it would all be happening too fast. The roads generally remain the same; the difference is your preparation for whatever happens on the way. The helmet of mindful behaviors helps you calm your mons and curb your urges so you can go through life without the weight of your eating disorder and emotional triggers on your shoulder.

Honing Your Commitment

When you commit, it is considered a pledge made for a course of action. In your case, your commitment is to the mindful behaviors you decide to practice. This pledge is maintained through steady practice as often as you are able to, and over time, you will find yourself doing it more often or even every day. When you decide to practice mindful eating, you need to choose to follow this path to the letter because there are no shortcuts or in-betweens. Persistence is also another very important feature of commitment. If you intend to achieve anything of great value, you need to stick to key commitments. A lack of commitment can make you open to falling off the wagon. Sometimes this can be okay assuming you get back on track when you notice you've digressed but other times, distractions can be really bad because they take you as far away from your practice as you can go and before you realize it, your enthusiasm to go back will be almost nothing. So how do you make and stick to a commitment? I'll be honest; there are no shortcuts to this. To make and keep a pledge, you have to work hard. Do you have that one friend who always makes New Year resolutions and is actually enthusiastic about them for the first week, but after that, they're completely unbothered? You think they just decided to let it go, right? That's not the whole story. They were enthusiastic about it but for the first three days, the rest was a struggle and at the end of the first week, they realized they couldn't continue like that so they let it go. Committing is step one. Trying and trying is step two. Choosing to eat mindfully isn't a walk in the park because it is going to feel like you're rewiring your brain, and sometimes you might fail to eat mindfully sometimes but that teeny tiny failure doesn't mean you can't get back on track forever. Let's say you decide to stop taking chocolate. You have an amazing first few days but after two weeks, you decide to take a walk after a heated phone call with your brother. You walk past a shop with a beautiful bar of your favorite chocolate on display, and without a second thought, you're already at the cashier with the chocolate bar in your hand. You wolf down the bar right there in the shop as quickly as you can and throw the wrapper in the trash can. However, as you walk out of the shop, you begin to feel like you've failed and might as well give up on the entire plan already. That probably sounds like the most logical thing to do, right? I mean, why waste your time?

Rather than giving up, acknowledge that you have been sticking to this commitment for two whole weeks. That's fourteen days without chocolate. That sounds pretty amazing to me. Fourteen days out of fifteen, that's a win to me. You need to appreciate your own efforts. Be kind to yourself. Keeping a commitment is especially hard in the face of your emotional triggers. After a rough day is a good example. When things are not going according to plan, the last thing on your mind will be to get some food and eat slowly so you can savor the taste and relish your experience, which ironically is the exact thing you need right now. Difficult days stretch the boundaries of your commitment to your initial decision to practice daily and annoyingly enough, these so-called difficult days hit you consequently so while you're recovering and rejoicing for jumping the first hurdle, another one hits you, BAAM!

The long and short of all I've been going on about is that you need to choose to commit every single day actively but even if you don't, even if you had every intention of following through but for some unfortunate reason, you couldn't, no need to come at yourself aggressively. Instead, approach the situation with acknowledgment, curiosity and acceptance. Whatever happened, happened. You wanted to eat mindfully but you couldn't, why? What emotionally triggered you to lose your footing? What do you think about these questions right here? What do you intend to do now?

Mastering Self-Discipline

Discipline means a lot of different things to a lot of different people. To some, it has some negative meanings and is kind of a turn off which is really disappointing because discipline is a vital aspect of maintaining a healthy lifestyle. I consider self-discipline a superpower because it is the uncanny ability to push yourself to perform a certain task despite your current negative emotional state. Think about all the things you can achieve if you had perfect self-discipline. There would always be a sense of knowing that anything is possible if you just put your mind to it. Imagine you decided to learn a particular skill, say horse riding. All you would need to do is decide to learn it and you'd be sure to follow the necessary steps to ensure you learn it. This example and many others, explains just how far the power of self-discipline goes and why it is a must-have in your skillset. A tiny thing to note is that discipline, all by itself, can create a sense of automated clinical action, almost even cold and completely lacking in emotion. So if you mix that with your helpful intentions, you can create for yourself a steady source of inspiration for your practice of mindful behavior.

Let's look at a few tips for boosting your self-discipline levels to help your mindful eating exercises:

1. Forgive yourself whenever you make a mistake. Don't forget; mindful eating is a long term practice with long term benefits so you don't have to drop it because of a tiny or even large lapse. If you don't do it right the first time, understand why and try again using a different approach.

2. Take things very slowly. Studies have shown that willpower can be compared to physical muscle strength. It can get exhausted and overuse if you don't give it a rest at some point during the day, and just like a muscle, it can be strengthened over a period of time, so do go trying to turn your life around in a single day. You should start with the littlest things and work your way up from there.

3. You will need belief in yourself to do this because what's the point of attempting something you don't even think you can achieve. No matter what other extra illness 9r disorder you suffer from, if you believe you can practice mindful eating, you can. All you need to do is make a commitment and believe you can stick to it.

4. Don't be afraid to ask for help. If it will help you feel better or make you comfortable, request a friend or family member to do it with you when they can. You can also consider signing up for support groups.

5. Acknowledge and appreciate yourself. You might have been beating yourself up at every little slip-up. How about you slow down a bit and appreciate the progress you've made so far? Give yourself a nice pat on the back for the days you practiced; those are the ones that count. A little pat on the back can mean a nice treat or a little gift to yourself.

Chapter 10

Simple Guidelines for
Mindful Eating

Mindfulness is pretty much a skill like others that can be learned through persistent practice. This skill doesn't give us any new ability per se. It just awakens the awareness that already exists within each of us. This awareness is normally a dormant ability that only comes alive in certain 'peak moments.' However, we can always wake up that which lies latent within us. It can be directed to different aspects of life, even eating. Mindfulness can be mastered through short intermittent moments of steady focus on our experiences. Here we will be exploring guidelines for mindful eating:

Slow Down

Americans have been noted to eat really quickly. A lot of people have reported that they just want to eat quickly and get it over with. This American attitude towards food isn't a new development. It has been recorded that foreigners who paid visits to American taverns centuries ago were dumbfounded at the speed at which food was consumed. This feeding technique was called the three Gs, and it stands for gobble, gulp and go. A historian, all the way from Tennessee, wrote in his journal that a visit to the colonies showed the attitude of haste, hustle and starvation displayed by inn regulars. He was puzzled at the speed at which people stuffed their faces. Another European who visited America in those times recorded his amazement at witnessing a lot of fast-paced eating in his inn.

This eating habit hasn't reduced over the years. In fact, it only got worse. Studies have revealed that North Americans eat lunch at a restaurant in just eleven minutes, and at the cafeteria in their places of work, they eat for eighteen minutes. Americans have been noted to eat while doing other things like driving, standing up or even walking. They're prone to eating and performing other activities at the same time. It's almost as if the food is in their way and they want to deal with it as quickly as possible. There are foods made for this eat-on-the-go purpose. Foods yogurt can be eaten comfortably while driving. All you need to do is squeeze one end of the tube with one hand and drive with the other. There are even adult bibs that are made for eating on the go so we don't spill the contents of our food unto our work clothes.

In a lot of European and Asian countries, however, this eating habit is seen as plain barbaric and very shocking. I have heard stories of the eating attitude of the French. In a typical French restaurant, the process of browsing through the menu in careful search of what to eat takes over thirty minutes. This is the time to discuss with the waiter and ask all the necessary questions about the food possibilities before finally settling on a choice. The restaurant manager and waiter would take offense if you just glanced at the menu and quickly picked something. The chef would take offense if you simply ate the food mindlessly while performing another activity like going through your phone. To them, a meal is almost like a ritual where the pleasure doesn't just come from the food itself but from the anticipation of the food and the accompanying drink. The only appreciation required by the chef, wait staff and manager is proper attention to food and drink. This is more to them than any amount of money.

The Japanese consider eating while walking really good manners. It recently became somewhat acceptable to eat and walk at the same time in Japan, and this isn't allowed for all kinds of food. It is just restricted to ice cream cones and this is because it will melt. All other meals and drinks are expected to be mindfully eaten while being seated. There are surely fast food shops that sell things like steamed filled buns, fried chicken, and hot potato croquettes, but the food is never eaten on the go. Instead, it is taken home, out on a dish, sometimes garnished and properly eaten mindfully.

How to Reduce the Fast Pace of Your Eating and Drinking

Learn to pause

Some helpful methods for pausing while learning to eat mindfully are:

- Before digging in, pause to observe each and every food item, taking note of colors, shapes, textures, and arrangement on the bowl.

- When that is done, show gratitude. Take some time to appreciate the animals and plants that ensured you would be eating the food. Thank the people who made sure the food got to you. Be thankful because food is a gift.

- Dig in then pause to appreciate the smell of the food. Think of it as part of the nourishment.

- Ever watched a wine connoisseur in action? You should eat like that. Breathe in the fragrance, then put a small bite in your mouth, rolling it around in your mouth. Savor every taste. If you can, try to detect as many Ingredients as you can. Now chew slowly and proceed to swallow. Drink some water to rinse your palate, and when your mouth is void of food and all flavors, start from the top.

- If you catch yourself eating without savoring the food, take a moment to stop and observe the food one more time.

Fletcherize

Once upon a time, the food blender was called the "fletcherizer" after a man called Horace Fletcher. Fletcher, in the twentieth century, gave speeches about how properly chewing his food helped him lose weight and become healthier. He proposed that each bite should be chewed thirty-two times. If thirty-two seems like a feat, you can try fifteen to twenty-five chews before swallowing. Pay attention to the changes in texture as you chew. Also, keep track of the time required to eat this way. You should start with just one meal a day i.e., chewing slowly during one meal every day. Over time, you'll find yourself doing this for more meals in a day until you unlearn the bad habit of mindlessly bingeing on your food. This method should be practiced especially when you're hungry and feel like you could eat a whole gorilla. You need to take deep breaths and munch on your food really slowly before swallowing. Each time you swallow, you can think of it as a nice gift you're giving to your tummy. Do this regularly and watch yourself begin to control your eating sprees actively

Drink slowly

Usually, when we drink anything, we don't really taste them which really defeats the whole point of the flavor. This results in drinking more just to get those brief sensations when we can just slow down and taste it. There are two ways to drink slowly. One is by keeping the liquid in your mouth for a few seconds and then swirling it around before you swallow. This way you enjoy and taste the drink. The people that certain advertise drinks do it perfectly.

The other way is to drink, put the cup down, taste, and wait until the flavor fades to repeat the process. This way is very simple and very reliable. You get to enjoy the taste and slow down at the same time. You can also do this while eating. Put some food in your mouth then drop the spoon into bowl. Don't even think of picking up your spoon until you have properly chewed and swallowed the one in your mouth. If you want to appreciate the feel and taste of the food in your mouth, close your eyes as you focus on the food in your mouth. When that one has been properly tasted and sent down your throat, you can proceed to pick up your spoon, put food in your mouth and drop it again. Pay attention to the interesting reactions your mind gives while you practice this.

Eat with your less dominant hand

This can be pretty tricky to do if you're ambidextrous, i.e., you can use both hands very well. Anyway, this method requires you eat with your less dominant hand on purpose. This means that if you use your left hand to eat and do other things, you will need to switch to your right hand for about a week. Doing this can be quite funny sometimes but very helpful even for issues completely unrelated to binge eating. This method trains your less dominant hand in general and also in preparation for things like a partial stroke or accident.

Use chopsticks

This method will enable you to slow down and pay more attention to every single bite. It is more effective if you haven't mastered how to use chopsticks just yet. Maybe it is one of the secrets of the Asian size. Have you ever tried bingeing on ice cream using chopsticks? You'll be in for a surprise. If you can properly use chopsticks, you can still attempt this method if you hold the chopsticks in your less dominant hand or dropping it after each bite.

Energy equation

This is another very effective method of mindful eating. This method is called the energy equation. Let it break it down. Food is considered a source of energy. This is because it is just sunlight that has been converted into various forms before becoming what we can actually consume. Whenever we eat anything of nutritive value, we are somewhat absorbing the energy of the sun, which we expend as we go about our daily activities. If bodyweight does not increase or decrease, it means that the energy we take in is equal to the amount of energy we burn. This is called an energy balance. If bodyweight decreases, surely the amount of energy lost is more than the energy absorbed. If bodyweight increases, it's the opposite. So how exactly do we get this energy? Whenever we eat or drink, we refuel. Unfortunately, calories cannot be absorbed by sleeping or just staring at food, unlike many people believe. You have to put it in your mouth for it to work and sometimes you have to get busy for it to be expended. Other ways the body uses energy for metabolism, thermo-regulations and insensible loss (which is energy loss during exhalation, micturition, shivering etc.)

There literally only two paths to weight loss. You either reduce the amount of energy you take in or increase the amount of energy you lose. If weight gain is your goal, there are also only two ways around it. You have to either increase the amount of energy you take in or reduce the amount you lose.

Despite how obvious this equation may seem, a lot of learned people are oblivious to it. This energy equation simply explains the normal changes in our body weight and hunger levels. A good example is how a lot of people realize they feel hungrier in the fall. This happens because the weather is colder, and the body is working overtime consuming more calories just to maintain the internal body temperature. The body requires more fuel and a lot more layers of clothing.

When you're seriously ill, rapid weight loss also happens because the body is burning more calories than you're taking in trying to fix you up. Another way you lose energy is through purging, so every time you go through the binge-purge cycle, you lose calories and put yourself at risk of many health complications. If weight loss is the goal, the best way to do this is to control the input and output of energy consciously.

Little changes do the most. Entering the middle age, you should do more of these:

1. Walking to shops that are within trekking distance instead of driving everywhere just because you can.

2. Choosing to park a good distance away from your destination.

3. Choosing to use the stairs every once in a while.

4. Cutting off soda and candy

5. Keeping your comfort foods with a member of your support system so that you can indulge only under strict supervision.

6. Buying frozen fruit instead of ice cream.

7. Purchasing tiny packets of chips if you must so that you can eat them in small quantities one at a time.

8. Eating moderate plate sizes ant first and asking myself if I need a second plate out of hunger or habit.

9. Digging into the main meal first, then waiting a bit to know if I should have dessert or not.

Out of Sight, Out of Mind

A lot of people, even binge eaters, are subject to the "fits of favorite foods" syndrome. This means that when you crave a particular thing say chocolate, you can have it steadily for about two weeks and then become completely uninterested after. I know a woman who lived and breathed chocolate but some years back, she developed an allergy to chocolate. What a cruel joke, right? Every single time she ate chocolate, she would get these blisters or ulcers in her mouth. You can imagine that she tried to find different ways around this. Then she settled for long periods of abstinence, which didn't even work because even something as tiny as a chocolate chip would riddle her mouth with blisters. She felt so deprived of her only comfort food at the time. Anyway, one day, she found that Reese's pieces contained zero chocolate. She was extremely happy when her husband came home with a large bag of it and put it in her desk drawer. It started with only a few pieces once in a while and eventually, it grew to handfuls. Guess what grew along with it… she did. She put on a whole five pounds due to binge eating Reese's pieces. She decided to observe her actions and how these cravings worked. She realized that the bag being within her reach was the problem. Whenever she sat at her desk to work, she would be so stressed, begin to see images of the bag in her head, and automatically reach for the bag. She also noticed that the amount of distance that she put between herself and the bag greatly affected her desire to munch on the contents. She decided to move the bag to her husband's office down the hall and this made her reluctant to go to his office every time she felt an urge, so ultimately, she binged less and with time, the images disappeared from her mind. The cravings gradually lessened and now she can look at them without wanting to stuff her face. She became mindfully aware of her problem and decided to observe with curiosity, and ultimately, she fixed it with time, patience and effort.

Chapter 11

Support Systems

We'll start with the simple things like what a BED support system is. This consists of a group of significant people, sentimental places and sometimes, animals that can help you when you are actively on a treatment plan out of the binge universe. Your support system can come in handy when you are having a difficult moment, a stressful day, or pent up emotions that you'd rather not binge away. There are so many ways a person can show care and support to a person with BED and there are also different kinds of support a binge eater can need and this depends on the kind of trigger they are dealing with.

Components of a Binge Eating Disorder Support System

Literally, anyone you want can be a member of your BED support system. If a person's value to you is of significance and they are supportive and more than happy to be your shoulder to lean on in times of difficulty during this journey, don't feel scared or ashamed to ask for assistance. A lot of binge eaters rely on family members and friends to make up their support systems. Others look to Internet buddies, work colleagues etc.

It is possible to get so overwhelmed with your urges and symptoms that you feel like you'd rather not have support from a person this time. Sometimes, places that hold sentimental value and pet animals can also make up your support system. A nice walk to your favorite place or some quality time with your dog or cat might be all you need to soothe your nerves. It feels just as good as talking to a person.

How to Form a Binge Eating Support System

Talking to your binge eating support system is usually the best bet, but finding them is the trick because forming a team of people who will be dedicated to your recovery isn't a small feat. The good thing is, I happen to have a few tips.

1. **Compile a list of support people in your life:** This requires you making time to think and write down the names of people who have supported you in one way or another in the past. If you like, you can also write down how exactly they supported you because this gives you an idea of the kind of support the person is capable of rendering to you. The person who helps with your laundry is different from the person who lets you vent at 2am.

2. **Compile a list of sentimental places and animals that have helped you better handle your emotions in the past:** For some people, a walk in the park is very calming while for others, the beach is the wonder worker. You need to pick your calm spots and write them down. Write down a list of

animals that calm you; you might be needing a trip to the pet shop.

3. **Compile a list of the health care professionals you know:** This obviously includes a BED therapist, then a nutritionist, a gastric surgeon, etc. If you don't know any, then thank heavens for the internet.

4. **Speak to the people on your list:** Asking them if they're okay and comfortable with being on your support system is very important because you need to know for a fact that they will be there when you need them. Dogs don't usually require asking, but you might want to check in with your cat.

5. **Use your support system:** Having a support system is one thing; using it is another thing. Remember this.

6. **Be thankful:** When they help you, be sure to help back when they need it. It can be as simple as helping to plan a surprise party or buying a nice gift for a relative. Make sure they know you value them as people and for their support.

Supporting a Loved One with BED

Family members and friends of binge eaters always seem to find themselves in a difficult spot because their good intentions can be easily misunderstood, and their comments about things like the binger's size or food preferences or actions can be an emotional trigger for the urge to stuff their faces.

Shame is one of the major triggers and is most affected, even unintentionally. Fear, anger and resentment are following closely. The family member or friend does not even have to be really critical or even judgment at to trigger these emotions. This is because a person who already feels ashamed about their body or their eating habits will be easily affected if and when these topics are brought up. Sometimes a harmless comment such as "you ate less than normal today" or "you've lost so much weight," which might even be intended as a compliment, might make the binge eaters feel ashamed of former bad eating habits. Binge eaters are super sensitive to people trying to control their body or eating habits and the urge to eat is likely to arise and the binge eater is likely to succumb to that feeling. They might end up eating compulsively because they're feeling hurt and rebellious.

Family and friends who would like to be helpful can start by having a calm conversation with the person with BED. You're just trying to talk, okay? You should begin by expressing your need to help and just ask if there's anything you can do or say to help **if** you notice they're falling off the wagon. You can go as far as suggesting activities you can do together like mindful meditation to calm the person when they begin to feel overwhelmed by their emotions, or you can decide to go on a walk with them or play a fun game you know they like. Each binge eater is different but it is agreed that a completely genuine desire to help in the absence of spite or judgment can go a long way in keeping their symptoms in check.

Conclusion

Binge eating disorder is a widespread disorder that is slowly making it into mainstream media with women as the primary focus, but no one is immune to the claws of BED. Learning to better handle and redirect emotions are one of the trusted ways to curb binge urges. The path to this binge free life leads through mindfulness. Mindfulness is a pretty simple practice but it isn't as easy, especially in the beginning stages. The simplicity lies in the act of paying attention and self-awareness. The difficult part is the self-discipline bit needed to practice and maintain this super helpful behavior steadily. Mindful eating will require you to have faith in the process and yourself despite how impossible the feat might seem.

In the end, it won't matter how difficult mindful behaviors were in the beginning. It won't matter how bored you get sometimes or how often you get wracked with confusion because, more often than not, you will have a deep connection to a powerful aspect of yourself. You will feel more aware of your thoughts, feelings and actions which gives you the upper hand when it comes to dealing with binge eating disorder and life in general. Self-awareness is a beautifully mysterious part of human existence that is still beyond the comprehension of scientists and researchers. It has always been there and it always will be. It lies at the root of your existence, always shining and always full of a sense of knowing. If you happened to find yourself lost in thought or stuck in the deep dark waters 9f the most frightening emotion you have ever felt, you would remain calm because, on some level, you are completely aware of everything that goes on inside and outside of you. I believe in you.

References

American Psychiatric Association. Diagnostic and Statistical Manual of Mental Disorders, Fourth Edition, Text Revision (DSM-IV-TR). Washington, DC: American Psychiatric Association, 2000.

Avena, N. M. "Examining the Addictive-Like Properties of Binge Eating Using an Animal Model of Sugar Dependence." Experimental and Clinical Psychopharmacology 15, no. 5 (October 2007)

Avena, N. M., P. Rada, and B. G. Hoebel. "Evidence for Sugar Addiction: Behavioral and Neurochemical Effects of Intermittent, Excessive Sugar Intake."Neuroscience & Biobehavioral Reviews 32, no. 1 (2008)

Avena, N. M., IP Rada, and B. G. Hoebel. "Sugar and Fat Bingeing Have Notable Differences in Addictive-Like Behavior." Journal of Nutrition 139 (2009)

Barnhill, John, MD, and Nadine Taylor, MS, RD. If You Think You Have an Eating Disorder. New York: Dell Publishing, 1998.

Beaver, John D., Andrew D. Lawrence, Jenneke van Ditzhuijzen, Matt H. Davis, Andrew Woods, and Andrew J. Calder. "Individual Differences in Reward Drive Predict Neural Responses to Images of Food." Journal of Neuroscience 26 (May 2006)

Begley, Sharon. Train Your Mind, Change Your Brain: How a New Science Reveals Our Extraordinary Potential to Transform Ourselves. New York: Ballantine Books, 2007.

Christine R. Maldonado, and Pamela K. Wauford. "Combined Dieting and Stress Evoke Exaggerated Responses to Opioids in Binge-Eating Rats." Behavioral Neuroscience 119, no. 5 (October 2005)

C. and John M. Neale. Abnormal Psychology. 8th ed. New York: John Wiley & Sons, 2003.

Dum, J., C. Gramsch, and A. Herz. "Activation of Hypothalamic BetaEndorphin Pools by Reward Induced by Highly Palatable Food." Pharmacology Biochemistry & Behavior 18 (1983).

Glass, Jay D., PhD. The Animal Within Us: Lessons About Life from Our Animal Ancestors. Corona Del Mar, CA: Donington Press, 1998.

Goldberg, Elkhonon. The Executive Brain: Frontal Lobes and the Civilized Mind. New York: Oxford University Press, 2001.

Gurian, Michael. Nurture the Nature: Understanding and Supporting Your Child's Unique Core Personality. San Francisco: Jossey-Bass, 2007.

Hagan, M. M., P. C. Chandler, P. K. Wauford, R. J. Rybak, and K. D. Oswald. "The Role of Palatable Food and Hunger as Trigger Factors in an Animal Model of Stress-Induced Binge-Eating." International Journal of Eating Disorders 34 (2003): 183-197.

Heller, Tania, MD. Eating Disorders: A Handbook for Teens, Families, and Teachers. Jefferson, NC: McFarland & Co., 2003.

Johnston, Anita, Ph.D. Eating in the Light of the Moon: How Women Can Transform Their Relationship with Food Through Myths, Metaphors, and Storytelling. Carlsbad, CA: Gurze Books, 1996.

Katherine, Anne. Anatomy of a Food Addiction: The Brain Chemistry of Overeating. Carlsbad, CA: Gurze Books, 1991.

Miller, Peter M. Binge Breaker: Stop Out-of-Control Eating and Lose Weight. New York: Warner Books, 1999.

Moe, Barbara. Understanding the Causes of a Negative Body Image. New York: Rosen Publishing Group, 1999.

Normandi, Carol Emery, and Laurelee Roark. It's Not About Food: End Your Obsession with Food and Weight. New York: Berkley Publishing Group, 2008.

Reba-Harrelson, L., A. Von Holle, R. M. Hamer, R. Swann, M. L. Reyes, and C. M. Bulik. "Patterns and Prevalence of Disordered Eating and Weight Control Behaviors in Women Age 25-45." Eating and Weight Disorders 14, no. 4 (December 2009).

Walsh, B. Timothy, MD, and V. L. Cameron. If Your Adolescent Has an Eating Disorder: An Essential Resource for Parents. New York: Oxford University Press, 2005.

Welch, C. C., E. M. Kim, M. K. Grace, C. J. Billington, and A. S. Levine. "Palatability-Induced Hyperphagia Increases Hypothalamic Dynorphin Peptide and Levels." Brain Research 721, (1996).